NERD FAITH

60 Second Sprints of Spiritual Guidance for the Occasionally Uncool

Rachel Kessler

For Amanda
and Martin

Morehouse Publishing
19 East 34th Street
New York, NY 10016
www.churchpublishing.org

Morehouse Publishing is an imprint of Church Publishing Incorporated.

Cover design by Emma Elzinga
Typeset by Westchester Publishing Services

ISBN 978-1-64065-887-5 (paperback)
ISBN 978-1-64065-890-5 (eBook)

Library of Congress Control Number: 2026930219

More Praise for *Nerd Faith*

"Full of wonder, encouragement, and nerdy sci-fi and fantasy references, Kessler does a bang-up job of delivering ancient truth to a modern world. Whether you are cautiously curious about Christianity or a longtime weary traveler of the faith, these bite-size reflections are sure to become your favorite way to spend a few quiet moments."

—KC DAVIS, author of *How to Keep House While Drowning*

"Jesus knew the power of stories to challenge, motivate, and transform. So does Rachel Kessler, and in *Nerd Faith*, she brings diverse stories together in ways that will make you engage your favorite shows and novels devotionally and approach your faith with fervent fandom. The book is simultaneously fun and profound, lighthearted, and movingly insightful. It is an invitation to grow, to reflect, and to celebrate the stories and imaginary worlds that we sometimes compartmentalize off somewhere separate from our faith, and yet which are calling out to be integrated as part of our worldview and our walk."

—JAMES F. MCGRATH, Clarence L. Goodwin Chair in New Testament Language and Literature, Butler University, author of *Theology and Science Fiction* and *Beyond Deconstruction*

"Most Christian devotionals function as spiritual 'aspirin'—prescriptive drugs to help the hurried, hurting believer to hustle through their day. Not this one. *Nerd Faith* is a feast of thoughtfully curated, theologically rich delectables, lovingly served to tired, disenfranchised followers of the Way. No matter where you are in your faith journey, Rev. Dr. Rachel Kessler's words will find you as lanterns in a fog, pointing to new worlds of hope, meaning, and justice. This will be the first book I will recommend to anyone desiring an intelligent, inclusive, accessible entry point to recapturing anew the wonder of following Christ in a chaotic world."

—KEVIN WILSON, founder of Cross Culture Chai and author of *The Way of Chai*

"Rachel Kessler meets faith with curiosity, kindness, and joy. Playful without being shallow, this book offers concise spiritual reflections and somehow makes space for all of us—believers, doubters, and everyone in between. Page by page, she reminds us that wonder is not something we grow out of and is a beautiful reminder that faith can be curious, generous, and delightfully uncool."

—IRENE SANKOFF, Olivier Award–winning writer and Tony and Grammy nominee

"*Nerd Faith* is a delightful and playful way to explore faith and beliefs. I think there is something for everyone to find in Rev. Kessler's cultural references and her experiences of the divine. Her passion and humor shine through her meditations and reflections."

—Elizabeth Ashman Riley, author of *Rage Prayers*

"As a rabbi, I've long appreciated Rachel Kessler's TikToks for their honesty and depth. This book is a testament to what it means to be a person of faith with deeply held commitments who also understands that faith is, at its core, a mystery. Drawing on her love of sci-fi and popular culture, Kessler offers a generous and imaginative invitation to approach God with curiosity, humility, and wonder rather than certainty."

—Rabbi Sandra Lawson, executive director of Carolina Jews for Justice

"Reading *Nerd Faith* is like reading the best kind of sermon: Every chapter, every vignette, contains theological depths and intellectual rigor, all while being couched in accessible language and relevant cultural references. As a reader, I was taken in by the fun and the fandom; as a priest and preacher, I loved the wisdom that so clearly reveals the good news of our faith. I'll be coming back to *Nerd Faith* again and again—to inform my preaching and pastoring and to form my own spiritual practice."

—Leyla King, canon for Mission in Small Congregations,
Episcopal Diocese of West Texas, and author of
Daughters of Palestine: A Memoir in Five Generations

"One might think that transcriptions of 60-second sermons—from TikTok of all places—must be trite or simplistic. One would be wrong. In this collection of reflections, Dr. Kessler dives deeply into the wisdom of the Christian tradition, offering parables from geek culture much the same way Jesus used the culture of his day, to give readers the good news and call them to participate in it."

—Rev. Dr. Heather McCance, president, Atlantic School of Theology

"Reverend Kessler elegantly demonstrates how good science fiction, fantasy, and pop culture are not just escapes, but rather illustrations of our understanding of—and responsibility to—our world, our community, and ourselves. *Nerd Faith* will launch many reflections and conversations, bringing deeper meaning to binge watches and moments of delightful connection to sermons, and readers may discover that both 'nerd' and 'faith' can sometimes be synonyms for 'joyful.'"

—Sean Decatur, president of the American Museum of
Natural History, New York City

CONTENTS

HOPE "All shall be well" (Julian of Norwich, *Revelations of Divine Love*)

LOVE "Simply put, we are not in this alone" (*The Good Place*)

PREFACE

I have never been, nor will I ever be, a cool priest.

This was my objection on Shrove Tuesday in 2020 when one of my more irreverent students confiscated my phone to download the (then relatively new) app TikTok and make an account for me, aptly titled "The Nerdy Priest."

Then, as we know, came the COVID-19 pandemic outbreak and resulting global shutdowns. COVID hit us all in different ways. In the midst of my own vocational burnout as I prepared for sessions of Zoom church and attempts at socially distanced pastoral care, I finally started making videos on that neglected TikTok account as a bit of a creative outlet. While my first videos were mostly frivolous fun, I soon realized how much hunger there was for honest engagement from the Church. Strangers on the internet responded intensely to videos talking about my childhood fear of the rapture, giving space to ask challenging questions about Christianity, and openly supporting the LGBTQIA+ community.

I often joke that my screen name is truth in advertising. I am a priest. I am also a major nerd. In my previous vocational life, I was an aspiring academic specializing in early medieval literature. Now I just find myself prone to overanalyzing all the media I consume, from sitcoms to young adult fantasy novels to blockbuster movies. While social media has its downsides, I love that my platform has connected me to so many people who are willing to journey with me in the strange associations my brain makes between my faith and my various fandoms. This book emerges from those reflections.

Organized around the overlapping themes of wonder, faith, hope, and love, these meditations begin by inviting a spirit of awe as we ponder the vast mystery of God. How do we resist the temptation toward certainty? Are we sometimes afraid to let the divine be unsettling? The section on faith provides an opportunity to address common questions around "progressive" Christianity, as well as a chance to wrestle with controversial issues and passages in the Bible. Can we shift our thinking from considering "This must be true" to "Why does what we believe matter for how we engage with the world?" The third section wrestles with hope in a seemingly hopeless world. What does it mean to live into our hope now, not just in some longed-for future? How does our view of salvation change if we embrace a Christian hope that everything wrong in this world can and will be redeemed? Finally, the section on love touches on the practicalities of how we live in relationship with one another. What does love really mean, beyond a bland idea of "niceness"? How do we love in radical ways that break down systems of oppression?

These meditations have emerged from five years of work as an "internet priest" and a lifetime of checking wardrobes for doorways to Narnia. They reflect the questions I have wrestled with and the stories I have shared that have resonated with many—believers, nonbelievers, and those still exploring where they find themselves. The goal of this book is not to construct a coherent theological treatise but to present an overview of honest responses to questions many people are asking. This is not a list of precepts to memorize and produce on demand as part of a debate but rather one nerd's personal adventure in the awe-inspiring worlds that can be found in faith and fandom. One of the great joys in ministry is not leading people to the "right" answers about God but walking with others as they discover new facets of the divine. Growing in faith almost always means growing to appreciate God's infinite mystery. As we journey, I hope we can embrace the potential for whimsy and wonder in the world God has given us. Beyond all else, I hope that God is too big to be contained in any simple answers.

WONDER

"Look upward and share the wonders I've seen" (*Farscape*)

Farscape is the story of the all-American astronaut John Crichton who finds himself flung into a far corner of the galaxy where he joins the ragtag crew of escaping prisoners on the (living) spaceship *Moya*. Along the way, he makes enemies, forms friendships, and builds a family with the love of his life, Aeryn Sun. What truly sets *Farscape* apart from many other science-fiction series is that all of the aliens Crichton encounters are products of Jim Henson's Creature Shop. The sci-fi channel original TV series consequently brings that exceptional blend of chaos and creativity that can only exist with Muppets. The strangeness of *Farscape*'s "uncharted territories" captures a sense of simultaneous fear and wonder at discovering a world beyond one's imagination. The series tagline that

Crichton offers in the later-season opening sequence is, indeed, "Look upward and share the wonders I've seen."[1]

That line is reminiscent of a prayer in The Episcopal Church's baptism service that asks God to grant the newly baptized "an inquiring and discerning heart, the courage to will and to persevere, a spirit to know and to love you, and the gift of joy and wonder in all your works."[2] Faith is about looking upward to see the wonders that abound in creation. The work of ministry is to lean deeply into the mystery of God and, in turn, to invite others to share in that sense of God's presence breaking into the world. In that vein, let us begin the meditative moments in this book with a posture of *wonder*.

---

1. *Farscape*, season 4, title sequence, created by Rockne S. O'Bannon (2002; A&E Home Video, 2009), DVD.

2. Episcopal Church, *The Book of Common Prayer and Administration of the Sacraments and Other Rites and Ceremonies of the Church: Together with The Psalter or Psalms of David According to the Use of The Episcopal Church* (Seabury Press, 1979), 308.

"Inconceivable!" (*The Princess Bride*): Embracing Mystery

The Good News: God Is Inconceivable

"Inconceivable!"
"You keep using that word. I do not think it means what you think it means."[1]

The 1987 cult-classic film *The Princess Bride* features no shortage of quotable lines and memorable moments. In this brilliant scene, the criminal mastermind Vizzini (played by the incomparable Wallace Shawn) has exasperatedly watched as a series of events take place that he had arrogantly deemed to be "inconceivable" in his attempt to kidnap Princess Buttercup. It turns out to be quite conceivable that his ship could be followed in the dead of night. It is conceivable that Westley, our hero and Buttercup's true love, could scale the Cliffs of Insanity. Vizzini is eventually outdone by overly relying on his presumed undefeatable intelligence. In the end, is Vizzini's failure, as noted by Mandy Patinkin's Inigo Montoya, that he does not know the meaning of the word *inconceivable* or that his grasp of the inconceivable is just way too narrow? While Vizzini is undoubtedly a

1. *The Princess Bride*, directed by Rob Reiner (1987; MGM, 2014), DVD.

laughable character, he is also relatable. People so often want the world to be *conceivable.* We want the universe to fit into our expectations because that means it must play by our rules! The fact is that so much in the universe—and certainly in the nature of God—truly is *inconceivable.* We cannot control God with the right set of prayers, rituals, or beliefs. With our defined sense of right and wrong and desire for punitive justice, we often cannot conceive of God's desire to redeem the whole world. That might be scary on the one hand, but it is also most certainly the core of the Good News: God's redeeming love is so great that neither we ourselves nor the world are beyond the hope of salvation.

Loving the *Via Negativa*

Whenever I visit a certain beloved parishioner, he will, without fail, engage me in a conversation about Pseudo-Dionysius the Areopagite, a fifth- or sixth-century Neoplatonic theologian. While it might seem a bit of an esoteric pastoral conversation topic, we share Pseudo-Dionysius's love of *via negativa*, "the negative way," or the conviction that God is fundamentally unknowable. Jesus was quizzed by the scholars and priests, who demanded he articulate the two greatest commandments. Jesus responds: to love God with all our heart, soul, mind, and strength, and to love our neighbor as ourselves. This poses the question: What does it mean to love an unknowable God? How could loving an unknowable God be relevant to loving our neighbor? We may not always be *good* at loving the people we encounter day in and day out in our lives, but at least we grasp that commandment in practical terms. Loving God is a lot more abstract, precisely because God is so wholly *other* and, therefore, unknowable. Maybe leaning into that unknowability of God is what it means to love God as well as our neighbors.

The more certain we are, the easier it becomes to wield "righteousness" as a weapon against those we deem unworthy. The more we approach our love of God with this attitude of awe, the more we can approach the divine image in one another with true reverence and love.

Aslan Is Not Safe, but He Is Good 

It is one thing to love the unfathomable mystery of God. It is another thing to sit with the notion that God's goodness will always be just a bit beyond our grasp. There's a moment in *The Lion, the Witch and the Wardrobe* when the Beavers first introduce the Pevensie children to the figure of Aslan, who is—spoiler alert—literally Jesus. Upon learning Aslan is a lion, the practical Susan exclaims: "Ooh! . . . I'd thought he was a man. Is he—quite safe? I shall feel rather nervous about meeting a lion!" To this Mr. Beaver responds: "Safe? . . . Who said anything about safe? 'Course he isn't safe. But he's good. He's the King, I tell you."[2] How often do we desire God to be *safe*? How often do we want a God that fits neatly into our preconceived categories? A *safe* God may not challenge us. A *safe* God hates the people we want to hate. A *safe* God is the God we find in elaborately constructed theological systems that fall flat when held up against the messy complexities of human existence. A *safe* God makes sense, but that *safe* deity is also so very small. Thankfully, God does not play by our human rules and will always be just a little bit dangerous. We can't comprehend the divine nature. That's OK! Instead, our work is to be attentive to the presence of God's goodness in the world and to share it extravagantly.

2. C. S. Lewis, *The Lion, The Witch, and the Wardrobe* (Collier, 1970), 75–76.

"Don't Check Your Brain at the Door"

How could someone with a PhD in medieval literature be satisfied as a parish priest? Would I really be capable of communicating in a way that would be accessible to the "average" parishioner? How condescending those questions I received during preordination interviews were to those "average" people in the congregation. Aren't "progressive" Christians supposed to pride ourselves on our intellectual approach to faith? A common saying in many self-identified progressive churches is that to be a faithful Christian, one need not "check your brain at the door." In other words, identifying as a follower of Christ does not require adherence to dogmas that some judge as irrelevant or irrational, like the Holy Trinity or Jesus's literal resurrection. Do we sell ourselves short when it comes to the deep intellectual traditions in Christian theology? Those in leadership risk offering congregations a version of faith that does not actually challenge them. Rather than dismissing a doctrine such as the Trinity or the Virgin Birth as esoteric or outdated, how much more *interesting* is it to approach those teachings with curiosity—with, indeed, a sense of *wonder*! Maybe we aren't actually meant to *get* every point of Christian theology. Maybe "not checking our brains" means continuing to wrestle with the mystery.

"The Beauty of the House Is Immeasurable"[3]

Piranesi by Susanna Clarke follows a man we know only as "Piranesi." He is the sole inhabitant of a house made up of a series of seemingly infinite rooms, which he studiously catalogues. His only friend is known simply as "The Other." The

3. Susanna Clark, *Piranesi* (Bloomsbury, 2020), 245.

unfolding relationship between Piranesi, The Other, and this mysterious house becomes a moving meditation on the nature of reality. Do we approach the beauty of the world as a utility to be exhausted for our own selfish purposes or with a sense of awe? What do we lose when we see the world only as a means to our own ends and not an end in itself? How much more critical these questions become when we apply them to our faith! The danger of religion emerges when we seek to harness the mysteries of God to serve our own agendas or desire for power. In so doing, religious authorities and institutions risk abandoning the awe-inspiring transcendence of the divine. Instead, we might think of religion as dwelling within the inexhaustible wonder of God's being, the depths of which we can never fully comprehend, even as we continue exploring. The posture of wonder allows us to view the structure of religion with humility rather than arrogance. The more *knowledge* we acquire of our faith and religious traditions, the more we see how incomprehensible God actually is. That is the immeasurable beauty of the divine.

God's Chaotic Goodness

As a class of fantasy character, Paladins are often *insufferable* (unless written by T. Kingfisher). My issue is that Paladins must adhere to a strict moral code, typically identifying as "lawful good" in their moral alignment. I may be a priest, but I have no interest in the "lawful" side of the alignment chart. Give me "chaotic good" any day. Rather than following a strict set of rules for their own sake, being chaotic good is about following sets of values like generosity, love, and compassion. We might even say being chaotic good is a nerdy articulation of Aristotelian Virtue Ethics: the idea that acting ethically is about the cultivation of character, not following a list of rules. In all honesty,

I believe God, as revealed in the Christian tradition, is chaotic good as well. Certainly, we can imagine some rules in the context of our faith, such as the so-called "golden rule." Such rules are not ends in themselves, but they act more as a framework for how to model our lives in the example of divine love. A deeper articulation of Christian ethics appears in the fruits of the spirit: love, joy, peace, patience, kindness, goodness, gentleness, self-control. Doing away with a neat system of "rules" may sound easy, and progressive Christians are often accused of doing away with rules because we just want permission to sin. Doing away with defined, orderly rules, however, means we are called to the more disciplined work of living in communion with the goodness and love of God and the virtues in ourselves that reflect God's nature. The deeper we cultivate those virtues, the more we live into God's goodness, even if we do so a bit chaotically.

Keep Fairies Weird 

Far too often, so-called "romantasy" books end up featuring the same vaguely magical morally gray "fae" shadow kings. Truly, seeing "fae king" in a book description can be a turn-off. On the other hand, stories that lean into "fairies," rather than "fae," generally embrace the disarming *otherness* of these creatures—as in *Emily Wilde's Encyclopaedia of Faeries* by Heather Fawcett[4] or anything by Olivia Atwater. One of the most fascinating things about faerie stories is the common trope that fairies are unable to lie. That does not mean one can take their words at face value. Fairies will play with loopholes of language and exploit any potential ambiguity. This idea that

4. Heather Fawcett, *Emily Wilde's Encyclopaedia of Faeries* (Del Rey, 2023).

the "fair folks" will always be truthful but never trustworthy plays on the illusive nature of language and, indeed, of reality itself. Truth is often not black and white. At the very least, the full scope of truth will always be just a little bit beyond the scope of human comprehension or our ability to articulate it. From the lens of faith, perhaps we need stories of otherworldly creatures that are truly *other* to remind us that God is mysterious, though not as a capricious faerie lord. When confronted with an entity that is wholly *other*, we should be exceptionally wary of ever feeling like we have fully comprehended it.

Through the Eyes of a Child

The titular alien from Steven Spielberg's 1982 classic film *E.T. the Extra-Terrestrial* may be the greatest cinematic Christ figure. E.T. comes down to Earth. He performs healing miracles. He tells us to "Be Good."[5] Then he dies and comes back to life, followed by ascending back into heaven! It's hardly a hot take to claim *E.T.* is a masterfully crafted film that explores childlike wonder. When shooting the film, Spielberg famously angled the camera so that essentially every shot would be at the eye level of E.T. or Elliott, his ten-year-old companion. As the film moves toward its conclusion, we see more starkly the contrast between the relationship Elliott and his siblings enjoy with E.T. and the attitude toward the alien visitor from adults. Whereas Elliott, a lonely child coping with his father's recent abandonment of their family, sees in E.T. a potential friend, the various agents of the government see, at best, an object of scientific research and, at worst, an alien threat to humanity.

---

5. *E.T. the Extra-Terrestrial*, directed by Steven Spielberg (1982; Universal Pictures Home Entertainment, 2019), DVD.

Elliott opens his heart to E.T., while the grown-ups lock E.T. in hermetically sealed plastic bubbles. From a rational perspective, the behavior of the scientists makes perfect sense: E.T. *is* a potential threat who should be contained. All the same, that default approach to analyze, experiment, and explain cuts them off from actually knowing and experiencing E.T. in his weirdness and wonder. That wonder is the reason that Elliott and his friends get to fly with E.T. through the California sky (to the impeccable vibes of a John Williams score in the background) while the grown-ups are left dumbfounded on the ground below. What in our "grown-up" perspective might we need to abandon in order to embrace the openness of childish wonder?

Finding the Waymarkers

Years ago, my friend Alice and I walked the St. Cuthbert's Way trail from Melrose Abbey in Scotland to Lindisfarne Island off the northeast coast of England. A feature of public walking paths in Britain are the "waymarkers" that denote different trails—for St. Cuthbert's Way, we followed signposts marked with the cross of St. Cuthbert. As happens in the hills of Scotland during the early spring, one afternoon we found ourselves in a patch of fog so dense it became difficult to see the waymarkers. It was more than a bit unsettling to be on a remote hilltop, uncertain of our path. Eventually, my friend was able to see the next waymarker emerge from the mist. To this day, one of my favorite pictures from our trip is of Alice looking back at me with a thumbs-up and a huge smile after this significant victory. A few days later, we would end our pilgrimage walking across the North Sea at low tide to reach Lindisfarne, a process that involved carefully following a series of poles marking the "pilgrim's path" to avoid dangerous spots of quicksand. Celebrating the mystery of God is great, but it is true that our lives can at times feel like a trek through uncertain terrain. It would be so helpful to have clear signs appear to tell us the way forward at certain juncture points: which job to take, whether to go to grad school, when to end a relationship. The work of faith is the ongoing process of becoming aware of where we recognize God's presence breaking into our messy and mysterious world. The unknown is scary, to be sure, but we live in the trust that signs of God's presence have ways of finding us.

"Only a Sith deals in absolutes" (*Star Wars: Episode III–Revenge of the Sith*): Suspicious of Certainty

Conviction vs. Certainty

As someone raised on the original *Star Wars* trilogy, I am contractually obligated to dislike the prequels. That said, I see something compelling in how Anakin Skywalker's descent to the Dark Side is tied to his rigid black-and-white morality. When Anakin declares to Obi-Wan Kenobi, "You are either with me or against me," the older Jedi wisely responds, "Only a Sith deals in absolutes!"[1] It is worth digging into what that really means. In my gut, I do hold to some absolutes: the call to love, the commitment to justice and equality, the dignity of every person. These are the convictions that unapologetically form the core of my being. There is a difference, however, between the notion of *conviction* and that of *certainty*. Certainty traps us in a rigid frame of thought that creates little room for questions or doubt. Convictions, on the other hand, are the values that, ideally, guide us to deepen our connections with

---

1. *Star Wars: Episode III–Revenge of the Sith*, directed by George Lucas (2005; 20th Century Fox, 2005), DVD.

the people around us. Our convictions can and should run deep, but we can also remind ourselves to hold them with humility. There is a danger, however, in the absolutes of certainty, especially when grounded in a sense of our own *rightness* and *righteousness*. Morality cannot be reduced to a list of clear rules of right and wrong outside the complex reality of lived experience. Human beings are complicated individuals who cannot be easily assigned to the roles of "hero" or "villain." Our world is so much richer when we open ourselves to the shades of gray that we so often encounter. Clinging to absolutes may not be a literal first step to the Dark Side, but it does tempt us to see the world in stark binaries of black and white, right and wrong. When we allow ourselves to seek certainty over creating room for mystery, we inevitably settle for a shallower view of God.

Limits of the Enlightenment

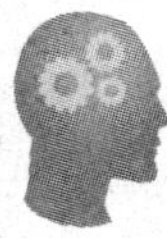

The central claim of Enlightenment philosophy is that all that knowledge must rest on sure and certain foundations. René Descartes, one of the seventeenth-century fathers of the Enlightenment, coined his famous phrase *Cogito ergo sum* ("I think, therefore I am") as the one truth he could know for certain. This changing basis of knowledge obviously led to great scientific innovations—10/10 to modern medicine! The Enlightenment and its quest for certainty, however, was also directly responsible for fundamentalism, or the reduction of one's worldview to core fundamental principles. In the sphere of religion, this produced obvious examples of fundamentalists who insisted on strictly literal readings of the Bible and hyperdogmatic approaches to faith. We also need to acknowledge the uncomfortable reality that fundamentalist atheists and fundamentalist Christians have more in common than either group wants to admit. Notorious anti-theist Richard Dawkins and your dogmatic pastor of choice have essentially the same view of the Bible. Both hold it to a standard of literalist original interpretation that the scriptures themselves do not claim and cannot support. Social media discourse has made it abundantly clear that certain anti-theists can be every bit as frustrating as the most antagonistic Christians, especially those atheists who assert that all religion is categorically evil. Such attitudes all too quickly devolve into Islamophobia, anti-Semitism, and rejection of indigenous spiritual practices. Whether we identify as theist or atheist, religious or spiritual, let us cultivate humility around the limits of the Enlightenment and the idol it makes of certainty.

A Lesson from Dr. Jones

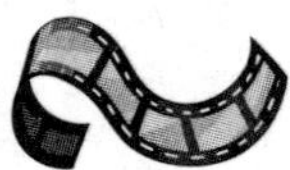

Harrison Ford's performance as Dr. Henry Walton "Indiana" Jones Jr. in *Indiana Jones and the Last Crusade* offered many viewers their first exposure to collegiate-style lectures. He infamously quips: "Archeology is the search for fact, not truth. If it's truth you're interested in, philosophy class is right down the hall."[2] While Indy's archeological methodologies might be open to critique, he is spot on in the distinction of *fact* from *truth*. Facts matter, to be sure, especially in fields relying on objectifiable data. In our Western worldview, we nevertheless privilege factual truth over different forms of truth, influenced as we are by the Enlightenment's quest for certainty. We dismiss, for example, the truth of stories or of art as less rigorous than an objectively verifiable fact. Conservative evangelical theology, with its

2. *Indiana Jones and the Last Crusade*, directed by Steven Spielberg (1989; Paramount, 2003), DVD.

literalist view of scripture and rejection of ritual, is especially susceptible to this bias to the detriment of more dynamic truth. For example, does the world need to have been created in six twenty-four-hour days for the creation story to be true? From the more Catholic side of the spectrum, arguments over how the bread and wine of the Eucharist become Jesus's literal body and blood can miss the more mysterious truth of how we ourselves become a part of the body of Christ by sharing in his body and blood. When our faith fails to make room for truth beyond objective fact, we end up building a faith on a faulty foundation. When we discover flaws in the scriptural narrative or church traditions, the whole system crumbles because our faith has not been trained to process according to different frameworks. Perhaps being taught (or even permitted) to ask the right questions of our faith in the first place allows it to grow stronger as our curiosity expands.

What Is Reality? 

Pan's Labyrinth is a beautiful but absolutely brutal movie about a young girl named Ofelia whose mother marries a vicious military commander in the aftermath of the Spanish Civil War.[3] Spoilers ahead! To escape the violence of her stepfather's home and to seek assistance for her mother's difficult pregnancy, Ofelia explores the woods around the estate. There, she discovers a magical faun who tells her she is a long-lost princess who will be reunited with her father in his kingdom upon completion of certain tasks. That's all pretty standard fairy-tale stuff. Ofelia's attempts to complete her tasks contrast with the horrors her

---

3. *Pans Labyrinth*, directed by Guillermo del Toro (2006; Warner Brothers, 2008), DVD.

stepfather inflicts on those around him. Ultimately, Ofelia's mother dies in childbirth. While Ofelia is able to save her baby brother, she is also eventually killed by the commander. The film ends with Ofelia as a princess being reunited (in heaven? in a fairy kingdom?) with her father. When I discussed the movie with others, one friend said, "How cool that all the fantasy was clearly in the girl's mind," while the other said, "How cool that the fantasy was so clearly real." Two very different takes on the story! But perhaps those two perspectives can coexist. As we reflect on different forms of truth, what does it mean for a story to be "true"? *Pan's Labyrinth* is a particularly harsh, violent film. The fairy tale Ofelia crafts in her mind may not be factual, but there is truth to Ofelia's love for her father. There is truth in Ofelia's desire to protect her baby brother. We might argue that such love is more true—more real—than the violence to which the commander clings to preserve his vestiges of power. When the world we must live in is cruel, stories of love and kindness keep us grounded in a deeper truth.

Holy History in the Holy Land

When I was in seminary, I took a pretty standard ten-day trip to see the major biblical sites in the Holy Land. Religious tourist sites, especially in Jerusalem, can be a bit much. Watching people jostle to be first in line to visit the site of Jesus's burial like they are fighting for FastPasses at Disney World is demoralizing, to say the least. I also found myself frustrated by the academic fixation on what we could know for certain about the historical reality of popular tourist destinations. What makes these sites in the Holy Land "holy"? Is it because we know factually exactly where Jesus walked, taught, preached, healed, or was buried and rose from the dead? Does that matter? Even as I felt myself overwhelmed by the kitschy, consumer-driven tourist industry that has grown up around Jerusalem, I also recall kneeling in one of the shrines in the Church of the Holy Sepulchre, noticing the grooves by an icon of Jesus. Those grooves had obviously been worn down by the fingers of pilgrims praying over the centuries. If there is a "holiness" to those pilgrimage sites, it comes from the holiness of the people who have prayed and continue to pray at them. There is a kind of magic that has seeped into those ancient sites that has little to do with our rigid certainty over the "facts" of history. We may never know where Jesus walked or where he was buried. We *do* know that for centuries, thousands upon thousands of pilgrims have flooded these sites with their prayers. To an even greater degree, as I have engaged with the Palestinian Christian community (the so-called "living stones" of the Holy Land), I am moved by the mystery of their ongoing faithfulness amidst the extreme oppression they experience. Holiness cannot be quantified, but it can be experienced in the legacy of shared devotion to which the Holy Land stands as witness.

Shifting Stories 

The Stardust Thief and its sequel *The Ashfire King* are the first two books in an underrated fantasy series by Kuwaiti American author Chelsea Abdullah. The books build off the foundation of *One Thousand and One Arabian Nights* to form a celebration of the power of story itself. Mazen, son of famed storyteller Shahrazad, is distressed by the conflicting stories he hears about a legendary djinni "Ashfire King." In addition to the stories, Mazen also knows this famous king personally—as Qadir, his friend Leyla's bodyguard—and he remembers his mother's words: "There is no such thing as a single truth."[4] Stories have real power. We do in fact create meaning by the stories we tell ourselves. Stories can carry more weight culturally than raw facts. People often respond defensively when their stories are challenged. In pursuit of a more equitable society, many of us are critiquing the default myths of American exceptionalism or white supremacy. As we rightly dismantle stories that built a national identity around myths of liberty and justice that never truly applied to everyone, we must build up new stories that center the voices who fought for true freedom. How do we make these stories ones that entice and persuade those who would otherwise be resistant? Like victorious Shahrazad who saved her life by drawing her would-be murderous husband into the web of her tantalizing tales, we might just change the trajectory of our world that desperately needs new and better stories.

Ways of Knowing

Traveling across hemispheres can mess with your sense of time in a big way! The time change was disorienting enough, but I was even more surprised by how much I was thrown off by the change in seasons. I planned accordingly! Knowing intellectually that it would be winter when I landed in Melbourne was very different from suddenly experiencing such shorter days and colder weather. Likewise, when it comes to matters of faith (or, say, the relationship between religion and science), it is important for us to remember that we do have different ways of knowing. Some knowledge comes to us intellectually.

---

4. Chelsea Abdullah, *The Ashfire King* (Orbit, 2025), 246.

Some knowledge comes to us through embodied experience. Faith is far more than the intellectual assent to a series of beliefs about the divine. Faith is richest when it emerges from our knowledge of God born out of our experiences of God—whether that is through traditional worship, encountering the divine in the love of a community, or embracing spirituality in the natural world. As more liberal or progressive Christians, we can sometimes get caught up in the intellectual side of our faith, which is great. That said, we do not have to be afraid that we are called to have a personal stake in our faith as well, especially when it comes to how we are called to live in relationship with one another.

On Prophets and Wormhole Aliens

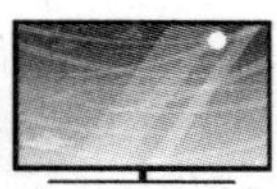

This may be a controversial opinion among the nerd community, but *Deep Space Nine* is fantastic: Gul Dukat as an all-time great sci-fi villain, Avery Brooks's performance as Commander Benjamin Sisko, or the friendship/*almost* queer relationship between Julian Bashir and Elim Garak the "simple tailor." The most fascinating part of *DS9*, though, is how the series deals with religion. *DS9* takes place on a space station located near an uncharted wormhole. Within the wormhole exist creatures known both as "wormhole aliens" to Starfleet and divine "prophets" to the inhabitants of the nearby planet Bajor. The disconnect between the worldviews of Starfleet and Bajorans forms much of the interpersonal tension of the series. As the series begins, the Bajorans have just emerged from a time of occupation, during which their faith was both a reason for their persecution and a source of strength in their resistance. Their identity as a deeply religious people becomes an ongoing source of conflict as they seek acceptance by the Federation.

Storylines explore how both the objectively minded Starfleet officers and the Bajoran religious establishment falsely believe their frameworks can fully explain beings that are beyond comprehension. While so much of science fiction pits religion and science in opposition to each other, *DS9* explores their resonance. These nuances come to the surface when the prophets/wormhole aliens select Commander Sisko as their "emissary." Sisko's reluctant journey toward accepting this role, despite his initial skepticism, is a running plotline through the series and offers a fascinating exploration of the intertwining of reason and faith.[5] What might we gain from allowing ourselves to see rationalism and wonder as complementary ways of viewing the world?

What Do We Worship? 

David Foster Wallace's "This Is Water" is arguably the most famous commencement address in recent decades. By chance, my husband and I were in the audience for the graduation at our alma mater Kenyon College in 2005, and to this day my husband will note that Wallace's words were so compelling he "even stopped reading his book to listen!" The speech begins with a joke about an older fish greeting two younger fish by saying "How's the water?," to which a younger fish replies, "What is water?" From there, the address goes on to offer a poignant reflection on embracing the beauty of the mundane and cultivating awareness of the invisible water of our lives in which we swim. One of Wallace's observations is: "In the day-to-day trenches of adult life, there is actually no such thing as

5. *Star Trek: Deep Space Nine*, created by Rick Berman and Michael Piller, Paramount Television syndication, 1993–97.

atheism. There is no such thing as not worshipping. Everybody worships. The only choice we get is what to worship."[6] Wallace goes on to describe worship as being caught up in a source of meaning outside ourselves. The danger of finding our purpose in something like money or success is that those ambitions will ultimately consume us. Worship in this framework is the water in which we swim. We might say worship is a kind of immersion, being caught up in a reality beyond our individual experiences. Wallace's words serve as a reminder to me that the core of religious belief and practice is not about being *right*, especially not at the expense of others. The purpose of our religious identity is to ground ourselves in meaning that is bigger than ourselves alone. May we ever be conscious of that water we are swimming through together in all the messiness of life.

---

6. David Foster Wallace, *This Is Water: Some Thoughts, Delivered on a Significant Occasion, About Living a Compassionate Life* (Little, Brown and Company, 2009), 98–101.

"I am a wonderful creature" (Old English Riddle): Wonder at the World

Frige Hwæt ic Hatte

A favorite unit for students in Introduction to Old English is always the Exeter Book riddles, a collection of ninety-nine short texts challenging the reader to puzzle out what object is being described.[1] Honey mead describes itself as being born aloft on bees' wings to become the scourge of humankind, toppling even the strongest of benches in the mead hall. The bookworm is noted for consuming texts without understanding them. Of course, we cannot forget the ever-fun "naughty" riddles. Often the riddles end with taunting "frige hwæt ic hatte" (ask what I am called!), as if the answer to the riddle will always remain just beyond the reader's grasp. Beyond anything else, these enigmatic texts celebrate a relationship to the world not yet sterilized by the disenchantment of modernity. The natural world exists not just for human utility or objective study but as an entity unto itself—as the wonderful mystery of

---

1. Many editions of the Old English texts and modern English translations of the riddles exist. I recommend both Craig Williamson's Old English edition and commentary in *The Old English Riddles of the Exeter Book* (University of North Carolina Press, 1977) and translations in *A Feast of Creatures: Anglo-Saxon Riddle-Songs* (University of Pennsylvania Press, 2011).

God's creation. There is both beauty and danger in that approach to the world. The world of the riddles comes alive with a spirit of playfulness. At the same time, there's a sense that, in these texts, the created world always exists outside the human ability to contain or control it. This sense of playfulness exists in texts written one thousand years ago. Wonder and whimsy are long-standing features of the human relationship to the world.

Points of View 

It's hard to conceive of a work that better invites readers to wrestle with wonder at our world than Samantha Harvey's *Orbital*. The short novel recounts twenty-four hours on a space station orbiting the earth, from the perspective of the six humans who reside on the station. These six individuals come from different nations with different backgrounds. As they circle the globe in their ninety-minute orbits, Harvey offers meditations on what it means to be human and our relationship to the planet below. There's a moment between mission specialist Nell, an atheist, and pilot Shaun, a Catholic Christian, where Nell asks Shaun how he can be an astronaut and believe in God. Shaun asks her how she can *not*. Nell looks out the window "where solar systems and galaxies are violently scattered. . . . Look, she'd say. What made that but some heedless hurtling beautiful force?" In response, "Shaun would point . . . at exactly the same violently scattered solar systems . . . and he would say: what made that but some heed*ful* hurtling beautiful force."[2] Harvey describes the difference between Nell and Shaun's perspectives as "both trivial and

---

2. Samantha Harvey, *Orbital* (Vintage, 2024), 66–67.

insurmountable." While it might seem at first that they have opposing views when regarding the vast magnitude of space, they each recognize that the scale of creation lies beyond our comprehension: whether we try to reduce creation to pure randomness or ordered design. Both perspectives are grounded in wonder.

Confronting the Wilderness 

In Becky Chambers's *A Psalm for the Wild-Built*, Sibling Dex, the nonbinary "tea monk," decides to leave their journeying along the beaten path between human towns and goes into the wilderness inhabited by robots, who have had no contact with humans for generations. Dex makes friends with the robot Mosscap, and what follows is a lovely exploration of what it means to be human. At one point, following Mosscap's lead, Dex reflects on the *intentionality* required to blaze a new trail in the wilderness. Dex cannot let their mind wander as they do when traveling a well-worn path. They must attend to the branches and roots blocking the way.[3] The abrupt shift Dex makes between the existing trail and the uncultivated wilderness serves as a reminder to the reader that we rarely interact with the natural world on its own terms. We have a largely sanitized relationship to nature. That is not an inherently bad thing. There is nothing wrong with seeking the security that civilization provides. At the same time, we would do well to acknowledge that our well-cultivated "civilized" way of life inevitably disconnects us from the natural world. We largely do not need to live in sync with the seasons. We have electric

---

3. Becky Chambers, *A Psalm for the Wild-Built* (Tor Publishing Group, 2021), 86–87.

lights that allow us to shape our days outside of the rhythm of sunrise and sunset. While trudging through the uncharted wilderness has its hardship, it does force Dex into an intentional awareness of their relationship with the elements of nature. How do we cultivate attentiveness to the wonder of creation? We are not separated from creation, but a part of it.

We Are Not Things

I often like to see the look on people's faces when I explain that my favorite movie is *Mad Max: Fury Road*. In addition to flaming guitars and brilliant practical effects, the film is a redemption story of reclaiming personhood. The villain of *Fury Road* is the warlord Immortan Joe, who hoards resources and reduces those in his compounds to literal objects, most notably the women he locks away to bear his sons. These wives manage to escape with the renegade Imperator Furiosa, declaring in the process: "We are not things." When we encounter Max in this setting, he is nameless. He has been captured and is being used as little more than a source for his universal donor blood. Max reluctantly falls in with Furiosa and Joe's wives. Through these relationships, he comes to believe there is value to his personhood and value to the ideal of community. The pivotal moment is when he finally tells Furiosa, "My name is Max," owning his humanity for the first time in the story.[4] It is a moment of transformation that leads to renewal, not just for Max but for the other characters with him. The film ends with the hope of community, where resources are shared, not hoarded, and where human beings are valued for

---

4. *Mad Max: Fury Road*, directed by George Miller (2015; Warner Brothers, 2015), DVD.

who they are and not the utility they can provide. It is tempting to see the world as a *thing*, especially living as we do in a society so enmeshed in capitalism and consumerism. Reducing the world—and our place in it—to its utility leaves us with an impoverished view of creation. When we celebrate the world and one another as sources of wonder, we become so much more than mere *things*.

The Way of Chai 

For the tea aficionados among us, Kevin Wilson's *The Way of Chai: Recipes for a Meaningful Life* is an excellent read.[5] Much like he does on social media (@CrossCultureKev), Kevin doesn't just offer inspirational chai recipes; he also talks about chai's communal nature. Chai is not just a beverage shared with a friend, but it is the mingled spices, flavor-steeped tea produced in the goodness of God's creation, and the fruit of labor from those who cultivated the leaves. Chai is communion in the truest sense, and we can think about this reflection in light of the images we see around food in Jesus's teachings. When Jesus performs his famous miracle of feeding the multitudes with the simple offering of loaves and fish, he criticizes those who are seeking him out because they experience this incredible miracle of feeding. On the surface, it seems that Jesus is criticizing the people by saying, "You just wanna follow me because you got your bellies full. Look for something deeper." It is important to note, though, that Jesus is calling the crowds to see the spiritual abundance provided through the physical abundance. In a world driven by consumption, it

5. Kevin Wilson, *The Way of Chai: Recipes for a Meaningful Life* (Tarcher Perigee, 2023).

is easy to become superficial consumers and miss out on this communion we are called to. As Kevin would point out, it is easy to accept Starbucks chai in place of the real thing. We don't have to be master chefs or perfect the art of homemade chai, but we can cultivate a spirit of intentionality in what we consume. The simple discipline of saying grace at dinner can be transformative. Even a meal of frozen pizza or mac and cheese can be an act of communion if we approach it with wonder and gratitude.

Beloved Bilbo (Not Baggins)

Shortly before I graduated from seminary, my priest said to me, "It's time you got a dog!" As it happened, a member at the parish of one of his friends had rescued a litter of puppies and he (correctly) marked me as an easy target to adopt one. I will never forget going to check out the puppies. As a friend later pointed out, no one just "goes to look at a puppy," and I came home with an adorable black-and-white border collie/beagle/lab that has now been a part of my family for fourteen years. In the process of the adoption, I kept asking the woman who had rescued my dog, whom we named Bilbo, and his siblings how much she was charging to sell the puppies. She kindly but firmly reminded me that she was not "selling" them. She was looking for homes to adopt them and was simply asking for compensation to cover the medical expenses she had incurred for them up to that point. I will always be grateful to that woman for reframing my perspective on bringing Bilbo home. Adopting a pet should not be the same as acquiring a consumer product like a set of bath towels or a new car. Bringing an animal companion into your life gives you the privilege of caring for one of God's marvelous creatures. Caring for the animal members of our families is a model of how we are called to care for and be stewards of all creation. Our pets also have an amazing way of reminding us that nature is weird and wonderful. Watching your dog sprawled out on his back with legs splayed out in every direction makes you realize nature is a bit ridiculous at times. Having the same dog lie across your legs on the couch while you watch a movie offers a sense of true joy, comfort, and companionship. Pets are truly a marvel.

On Being Cautious Travelers

We cannot talk about the wonders of creation or the notion of living in harmony with nature without also recognizing there is danger in the natural world. As a medievalist, I am unable to resist stories that critique our hypermodern concept that, with sufficient technology, humanity can shield itself from vulnerability to nature. One such book is *The Cautious Traveller's Guide to the Wastelands* by Sarah Brooks. This is a light fantasy set in the steam age where the only way between Asia and Europe is through a mysterious "wasteland" that consumes everything that dares to go through it. The central feature of the novel is the Trans-Siberian Express, an armored train developed by the strange "company" to traverse this most direct route through the wasteland. As we learn, however, the mysteries of the wasteland are insidious. Even looking outside the windows for too long can affect unwary passengers.[6] When I read a book like this, I immediately think of the tragedy of the *Titanic*, the supposedly "unsinkable" ship destroyed by grazing against a single iceberg. We might also

6. Sarah Brooks, *The Cautious Traveller's Guide to the Wastelands* (Flatiron Books, 2024).

remember the hubris of billionaires seeking the wreckage of the *Titanic* who were killed when their submersible exploded under the pressure in the ocean depths in 2023. It is the height of human folly to assume that with enough money or ingenuity, we can insulate ourselves from vulnerability to the natural world. This reality is all the more urgent for us to accept as we face the reality of human-manufactured climate change. *The Cautious Traveller's Guide* may be something of a cautionary tale, pun intended, but it is also quite hopeful in the end. In contrast to the ominous "company," the central characters learn to live in communion with the wasteland, not in opposition to it. The challenge for us is whether we see the natural world around us, in all its beauty and wildness, as an entity to be embraced and experienced, or comprehended and conquered.

Renewal, Not Recycling 

I have on occasion made the mistake in adulthood of reading my children the classic *Berenstain Bears* books that I loved in my own childhood. Several decades later, it has become harder to miss the troubled gender dynamics (poor Mama Bear really does have three children to raise with Brother, Sister, and Papa) or the fatphobia of stories like *Too Much Junk Food*. A book that did make me pause and think, though, was *The Berenstain Bears Don't Pollute (Anymore)*. Learning about the dangers of pollution, Brother and Sister take dramatic actions like starting an after-school club! Making signs! Picking up litter![7] There is a certain naive 1990s optimism of this

7. Stan Berenstain and Jan Berenstain, *The Bearenstain Bears Don't Pollute (Anymore)* (Random House, 1991).

approach to the stewardship of creation. All we need to do is "reduce, reuse, and recycle" to address the very real threat of climate catastrophe. In reality, the challenge we face will require far more from us. Our goal (especially in the most privileged parts of the planet) cannot be merely to modify ever so slightly our excessive patterns of consumption and remind ourselves to recycle. We cannot put the burden on changes to individual patterns of behavior while ignoring the impacts of governments and large corporations. We must fundamentally change our relationship to the natural world. Let us not forget that in the story of creation, God calls us to be its stewards in Genesis 1:28. Creation is a wonderful entity to be embraced with awe, not merely a resource to exploit. Shifting our default paradigm for thinking about the world is certainly daunting. It also fills me with hope for what our stewardship of God's creation might come to look like: our governments actually embracing energy over our worship of fossil fuels, an economy that stops promoting cycles of endless consumption, and more radically, an embrace of community where resources are shared rather than hoarded.

A Eucharistic Life 

One amazing theological quotation comes from the Russian Orthodox Priest Alexander Schmemann in his book *For the Life of the World*. Schmemann writes: "The only real fall of man is his noneucharistic life in a noneucharistic world."[8] What does that mean? The Greek word *eucharist* simply means "thanksgiving." For Father Schmemann, the "fall" or "sin" of

8. Alexander Schmemann, *For the Life of the World: Sacraments and Orthodoxy* (St. Vladimir's Seminary Press, 1973), 18.

humankind is our failure, fundamentally, to understand that the created world is a gift, one that we betray in so many ways. Seeing the world *eucharistically*—through the lens of thanksgiving—does not mean embracing a mindset of toxic positivity that ignores the brokenness of the world or the suffering that is all too present. Father Schmemann does, however, challenge us to see all of creation as a sacrament, or sign, of God's presence. There is no distinction in Father Schmemann's view between the *sacred* (holy) or *secular* (ordinary). Instead, places and rituals that we set apart as sacred are meant to help us see the sacredness of all things. This is particularly true with regard to the Eucharist itself, the ritual in which Christians share in bread and wine as a way of sharing in the literal or symbolic body and blood of Christ. Ordinary elements of bread and wine—the products of God's creation and the fruits of human labor—are offered up by the priest to be made *extraordinary*. I sometimes talk with my students about having "magic hands" as a priest, by which I lift up the bread and wine to be blessed by God and invoke the blessing of God's Holy Spirit upon them. For Father Schmemann, every meal we share becomes a reflection of this eucharistic offering. We are called to live at all times as priests of creation, recognizing there is no part of our lives that cannot be made sacred. Wonder exists all around us, even in the midst of the mundane, if we train ourselves to look for it!

"We're all mad here" (*Alice in Wonderland*): Wisdom and Whimsy

Limits of Logic

I have always had a love-hate relationship with *Alice in Wonderland*. On the one hand, this entire book resonates with my unapologetic love of the weird and wonderful.[1] As a kid who grew up obsessed with portal fantasy stories and hoping to find Narnia in every closet I encountered, I always thought Alice was rather ungrateful! Instead of embracing the *wonders* of Wonderland, Alice spends her time complaining and trying to make this world she has encountered fit into her rationalist nineteenth-century perspective. Rather than being willing to play by the illogical rules of Wonderland, she imposes her own logic on its madness. Admittedly, Wonderland might not be an entirely benign place. I do enjoy stories that play on the dangers inherent in such magical worlds, Melissa Albert's *The Hazel Wood* being an excellent example. Even these stories, however, tend to recognize an inescapable draw in places like Wonderland, Narnia, and the world of Oz. We know there are aspects of our existence that do not conform to rational rules. Logic cannot explain the

---

1. Lewis Carroll, *Alice's Adventures in Wonderland*, illustrated by Arthur Rackham (Sea Star Books, 2002), 76.

stirring of our soul at a beautiful piece of music. Rationality cannot explain the all-consuming love I have for my children. Our human nature cannot be reduced to what makes sense. We can pretend we are perfectly logical beings, or we can embrace that touch of madness in all of us that makes life that much more abundant.

Celebrating Ordinary Barbie

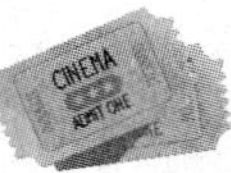

While the *Barbie* movie and America Ferrera's monologue about the complexities and contradictions imposed on women living under the burden of patriarchy was undoubtedly a highlight of summer 2023, what if we all missed something equally profound in the idea of "ordinary Barbie" proposed by Ferrera's character at the end of the film? Ordinary Barbie was key to the whole message of the movie! Every other Barbie was amazing in some way: Doctor Barbie, Lawyer Barbie, President Barbie. Instead of always looking away from ourselves to some kind of impossible exceptionalism demanded of us under patriarchy and capitalism, Ordinary Barbie challenges us to embrace the extraordinariness of ourselves, outside of our productivity or achievements.[2] I often challenge my overachieving college students to embrace mediocrity. That does not mean to give up on dreams or ambitions. We should have aspirations! But we are often tempted to define ourselves by what we accomplish. Let us embrace the idea that we are worthy by virtue of simply *being*. Our fundamental worth comes from who we *are* not what we can do. Our "ordinary" selves are made in the image of God. That is wondrous.

---

2. *Barbie*, directed by Greta Gerwig (2023; Warner Home Video, 2023), DVD.

In Defense of Disney Adults

I have come to accept that I am a Disney Adult (TM). Walt Disney World is my happy place, and I make no apologies for it. I can't help but think that much eye-rolling at Disney Adults speaks to a discomfort with embracing childlike wonder. We live in a *disenchanted* world, especially when it comes to notions of adulthood. Frankly, we look down on childhood and children in general. Children are often seen as an annoying burden, but children are inherently chaotic and unashamed of expressing their emotions. Adults who love the Disney Parks are generally unembarrassed about expressing unfiltered joy. Did my friend cry when she met Chewbacca at Hollywood Studios? Absolutely! That is Disney magic. Perhaps adults are drawn to something like Disney because we live in a world where there is very little whimsy. It should also be said that the Disney Parks fandom, like fandom in general, provides a sense of shared community, even ritual. There is a reason Disney cast member training includes a section on "traditions." Yes, it is ironic that many of us find that joy in the, admittedly, capitalist hellscape that is something like Walt Disney World. That is a valid conversation. In response I will just say: Disney World is also a place where we get to ride a dragon, fly the Millennium Falcon, and have dinner at a castle. If you are going to pay seven dollars for a soft pretzel wherever you go on vacation, it might as well be shaped like Mickey Mouse. At the end of the day, we might do well to embrace a bit of "cringe" in a world where we all try so hard to be "cool." Where do we make room for unapologetic joy in the midst of our mundane everyday lives?

Figment Deserves Better 

While I love Disney World, I am not sure that even in the fullness of Christian charity I can forgive the Walt Disney Company for destroying the single greatest ride in the history of Disney Parks. I mean the classic "Journey Into Imagination." The original attraction ferried riders into a genuine exploration of imaginative possibilities. Guests were guided by the whimsical inventor Dreamfinder and his assistant, the mischievous dragon Figment. As a child, I was captivated by the song that played in the background of the ride. We can all use the Dreamfinder's reminder about the power of "one little spark" of creativity to build a world of dreams.[3] It saddens me that my own children have only experienced the current iteration of the "Journey Into Imagination" with Eric Idle teaching about the five senses and a farting Figment. Apart from nostalgia for a diminished theme park ride, I can't help but feel the new attraction betrays the idea of imagination. Imagination is what calls us to conceive of a world *beyond* what our physical senses reveal to us. Imagination invites us into the idea of the mysterious and mystical, as the Dreamfinder in all his whimsy tried to teach us.

Imagining Anxiety 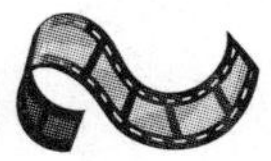

Let's talk about anxiety and imagination in *Inside Out 2*. Much like the original film, we see animated personifications of the emotions of now adolescent Riley. While the first film followed Riley through the stress of her family moving and starting a

---

3. Robert Bernard Sherman and Richard Morton Sherman, "One Little Spark–From Journey into Imagination," Walt Disney Records, 1982.

new school, the sequel picks up with the challenges of puberty. The second film introduces new emotional characters, such as Anxiety! As soon as Anxiety arrives, it decides that it should control Riley's brain. Hijinks ensue.[4] At one point, the other emotions enter Riley's imagination. There, they find not only Anxiety but also the creatures responsible for Riley's imagination bound up in cubicles, churning out all of the worst-case scenarios that could transpire in any given situation. Anyone with anxiety absolutely relates to this. As my therapist once said, "Anxiety is the curse of people with big imaginations." To which my husband replied, "But anxiety is also a limitation of imagination." His point is well taken. Anxiety can certainly cause us to *imagine* endless catastrophes; however, anxiety also leaves our imagination effectively imprisoned. We cannot always imagine solutions or move beyond the warnings our anxiety brings us. I am reminded of Jesus's ministry and how often he pushes his followers to see potential beyond fear, whether it be on a boat in a stormy sea or confronting demons. It's worth considering how often our anxieties limit us instead of pushing us to see potentially positive outcomes. Many of the most dangerous movements today are those rooted in that fear, driven by people who cannot see the potential of a more inclusive world. We must not let our anxieties rob us of hope!

It Has Pockets! 

It is a truth universally acknowledged that, should you compliment a woman on a dress that happens to have pockets, she will inevitably reply, "Thanks, it has POCKETS!" Has there been a greater revolution in women's fashion than the ubiquity

4. *Inside Out 2*, directed by Kelsey Mann (2024; Sony, 2024), DVD.

of pockets over the past decade or so? Whenever I ponder the popularity of pockets, I remember the 1935 Fred Astaire/ Ginger Rogers film *Roberta*, which follows American John Kent, who, for rom-com reasons, ends up running his aunt's high fashion dress shop, much to the consternation of his love interest, Stephanie. At one point, in order to get Stephanie to assert herself as the proper knowledgeable manager of the shop, John and his friend Hunk decide to design the worst dresses they can imagine. The most offensive feature: POCKETS! Stephanie is so outraged at their apparent incompetence that she agrees to resume management of the shop.[5] As a teenager watching the movie when pockets were still sadly hard to come by in my clothes, I was flummoxed as to why everyone in the film just accepted that pockets in women's clothes were a self-evidently bad idea. It may seem a little over the top to see the proliferation of dresses with pockets as a powerful sign of societal progress, but I do think pockets are significant! The power of pockets reminds us that even something as seemingly silly or whimsical as fashion can have a deep impact on the world. As women and femmes have assumed more positions of influence, we have been able to make a bizarrely specific change that has made our lives categorically better. Today, we gain pockets. Tomorrow, we smash the patriarchy.

---

5. *Roberta*, directed by William A. Seiter (1935; Warner Archive Collections, 2017), DVD.

We All Need a Harvey

> *"Years ago, my mother used to say to me, she'd say . . . 'In this world, Elwood, you must be oh so smart or oh so pleasant.' Well, for years, I was smart. I recommend pleasant."*[6]

The 1950 film *Harvey* is a must-see classic. Elwood is an eccentric man whose best friend happens to be a seven-foot invisible rabbit named Harvey. This unusual friendship causes no end of consternation to Elwood's respectable sister, who eventually tries to have him institutionalized for his failure to conform to societal expectations. In the end, Elwood's whimsy wins the day, as he walks off into the sunset with Harvey. One of the most impactful parts about *Harvey* is that Elwood's peculiarities are a choice that he has actively made. He could have chosen to pursue being "smart" according to the standards of the world. Maybe that would look like being cutthroat in business or avoiding leisure for the sake of accomplishment. Instead, he chose a life of simply being pleasant. *Harvey* makes a pointed commentary on moralistic ideals like respectability or even something like the "Protestant work ethic." Achievement and success are not valuable in themselves. They are certainly not anything that God calls us to pursue. We make meaning in life through decency, radical kindness, and, yes, being pleasant. That can be a countercultural choice at times, but it is certainly a choice worth making. It might just change the world.

6. *Harvey*, directed by Henry Koster (1950; Universal, 2001), DVD.

Life Is Pretty Epic 

The companies that lead tours of the Hobbiton movie set near Auckland and more rugged *Lord of the Rings* filming locations outside of Queenstown in New Zealand know their target demographic a little too well. All their marketing materials say things like "Put yourself inside the story!" or "Take a picture of yourself as an elf in Lothlórien!" For the record, yes, I did dress up as a hobbit in the Green Dragon. It was amazing and I have zero regrets. These tour companies have connected with something fundamental in human nature. We as human beings are creatures of story. We all have a need to be caught up in narratives that are bigger than just our own experiences. At its best, Christianity is not a set of beliefs about God, but it is a dramatic story about God's love for the world. One of my core beliefs that calls me back to Christianity in my inevitable periods of doubt (even as a priest!) is the idea that in the Christian narrative, it is God who steps into *our* human story. God chose to enter human history and to live and die among us. God chose to be revealed to us not in the power of divinity, but in the tangible vulnerability of humanity. We do not have to travel halfway across the world for a photo op on a movie set, as awesome as that was, in order to enter into a larger narrative. To be a Christian means to lean fully into that story of God's radical love for all of humanity in the ordinariness of our lives. We participate in that story every time we show love for the people around us and every time we advocate for justice in the name of the gospel. That's pretty epic.

In Praise of Puddleglum 

The Silver Chair is my favorite book in *The Chronicles of Narnia* for one major reason: Puddleglum the Marsh-wiggle. Fun fact:

Puddleglum is played by Doctor Who's fourth doctor, Tom Baker, in the BBC miniseries! As his name suggests, he is superficially a gloomy character who can always be counted on to see the worst in any given situation. Throughout the story, however, Puddleglum's blunt pessimism becomes a strange sort of optimism. When the two central human children complain about the blandness of their food, Puddleglum replies practically that if it tastes of nothing, it cannot taste terrible. Puddleglum's triumphant moment comes when he and the children have been captured, along with the Narnian Prince Rilian, below the earth by the Queen of the Underland. She tempts them to forget about the world above, capturing them under a spell claiming Aslan and Narnia are only myths. To this Puddleglum exclaims:

> *Suppose we* have *only dreamed, or made up, these things—trees and grass and sun and moon and stars and Aslan himself. Suppose we have. Then all I can say is that, in that case, the made-up things seem a good deal more important than the real ones. Suppose this black pit of a kingdom of yours is the only world. Well, it strikes me as a pretty poor one. . . . That's why I'm going to stand by the play-world. I'm on Aslan's side even if there isn't any Aslan to lead it. I'm going to live as like a Narnian as I can even if there isn't any Narnia.*[7]

As an adult, I see how disenchanted our world so easily becomes. I see so much bigotry born out of a sense that for anyone to win someone else must lose. I see self-righteousness born out of small-minded fundamentalism. Faith should challenge us to imagine a better way of living in relationship with one another. The grace of God surpasses our human understanding, even as we work imperfectly to strive to manifest that grace now.

---

7. C. S. Lewis, *The Silver Chair* (Collier, 1971), 159.

FAITH

"Believing takes practice" (Madeleine L'Engle, *A Wind in the Door*)

How many communion wafers does it take to make a whole Jesus?

These are the kinds of questions students text you in the middle of the night when you are a college chaplain. The answer is one. One whole Jesus in every communion wafer.

That was my first semiviral video when I started making content on TikTok. It may seem silly, but I stand by my answer: The fullness of Christ's presence is within every element of communion. That reply sparked off a lot of questions, some ridiculous, some profound. These video questions and replies became a fascinating way to enter into conversation articulating what it means to be a Christian, especially one who tries to think seriously about God, the Bible, and Church tradition.

Madeleine L'Engle, *A Wind in the Door* (Square Fish, 2007), 153.

Given that I am open about having deconstructed my very conservative background, some of the people who engage with my content online have assumed that I am an atheist, or at least on my way to becoming one. It comes as a surprise to them that I am, in fact, a Christian priest. More often than not, their reaction upon hearing I am specifically an Episcopal priest is something along the lines of "Oh yeah, but Episcopalians don't actually believe anything anyway." But we do! Our church very clearly affirms the confession of the Christian faith expressed in the Nicene and Apostles' Creeds. In my ordination vows, I confessed that the Old and New Testaments are the word of God and contain all things necessary for salvation. Christians like me and Christians from more conservative or fundamentalist traditions just have different conceptions of what we mean when we say the scriptures are the Word of God. In our baptism, we commit to *living* our faith through promises such as to seek and serve Christ in all persons and to respect the dignity of every human being.

Faith can be an elusive concept. We often mistake the idea of "faith" as the intellectual assent to a series of abstract propositional statements about God. This is incredibly problematic when we reduce the idea of "salvation" to belief, or lack thereof. Faith does not exist in a binary. I do not even think it is fair to say that faith exists on a continuum, with fundamentalists on one end and atheists on the other. Perhaps the most important thing to embrace about faith is that it can never be static. Faith is an embodied, lived reality. Faith provides the framework through which we understand the world and which shapes how we live in relationship with one another—whether we identify as "religious" or "spiritual" or none of the above!

The reflections contained in this section offer a glimpse into my faith and why I hold to the convictions that I do. What do I believe? How do I wrestle with doctrines like the

Trinity or the Virgin Birth? As I discussed in the previous section, no articulation of faith can ever come close to capturing the mystery and wonder of God, which will always surpass human understanding. My goal in this section is to share a bit of how my faith has grown and changed through my life. As you read these passages, I invite you to ponder the questions that arise. What does faith mean to you?

"Isn't it a little suspicious that the only true religion is the one with which we happened to grow up?" (Rachel Held Evans, *Faith Unraveled*): Deconstructing and Reconstructing

Thank You, Rachel

I can't talk about deconstructing my faith without paying tribute to the witness of Rachel Held Evans, a blogger and author who tragically died in 2019 at age thirty-seven. There's something wistful in being an "older" person creating content online watching a new generation of young people ask difficult questions of their faith and build a community around "deconstruction." I sometimes feel a sense of grief that such a community of shared experience did not exist when I was a young adult. What I did have was Rachel Held Evans's blog, and eventually her books like *Searching for Sunday* and *Faith Unraveled*.[1] Hers was

---

1. Rachel Held Evans, *Faith Unraveled: How a Girl Who Knew All the Answers Learned to Ask Questions* (Zondervan, 2010), 100.

the first voice I encountered who shared a background similar to my own and who was asking many of the same questions I did. How can we trust in a God who would condemn a child to hell who had not yet prayed the "sinner's prayer"? How does anyone actually take the Bible literally when we are always picking and choosing the passages we ignore and the ones we emphasize? What does salvation really mean? I will always be grateful for Rachel's witness to a faith that was at once bold in conviction and broad enough for questions. I strive to continue her work of witnessing to the God of abundant love, always holding to her words, "What makes the gospel offensive isn't who it keeps out, but who it lets in."[2]

"I Don't Want to Go Back to Your World" 

Please indulge me in one more reflection on the sci-fi series *Farscape*, specifically about the character of Aeryn Sun, played by the amazing Claudia Black. I am a so-called "exvangelical"—the term for someone who left an evangelical faith tradition. I may not be a kick-ass ex-soldier like Aeryn, but I relate to her journey out of a rigid, authoritarian background to embrace a life she never would have expected. Aeryn begins the series as a Peacekeeper, your standard sci-fi space fascist, but becomes exiled from her military unit and thrown in with our motley crew of convicts and misfits aboard the spaceship *Moya*. Aeryn goes through feelings of anger that she has been cut off from the only world that she has known and that provided her with rules and clarity. As the series goes on, through her experiences and friendships, Aeryn discovers a world that is bigger

2. Rachel Held Evans, *Inspired: Slaying Giants, Walking on Water, and Loving the Bible Again* (Thomas Nelson, 2018), 186.

than anything she had ever known. Eventually, she confronts the commander who first cast her out from her military unit. He is at her mercy, and she could force him to reinstate her in the life she lost. Instead, she declares: "I don't want to go back to your world!"[3] How many of us who have "deconstructed" from a rigid faith tradition can relate? It can be disorienting to let go of a system that provides us structure and rigid answers about right and wrong. In the pilot episode of *Farscape*, our protagonist John Crichton encourages Aeryn to leave the Peacekeepers, with the promise that Aeryn "can be more." Deconstruction is scary, but it is also not an ending. We can rebuild our faith into something so much more than it once was.

Martin Luther Needed a Hug 

Martin Luther, father of the Protestant Reformation, is a fascinating historical figure. It's kind of wild that the trajectory of the Western church for the last five hundred years comes down to one guy and his deep anxiety for the state of his soul. That salvation anxiety ultimately led to the reformation of the entire church! If you're less familiar with Luther's history, he was a student of law who had a dramatic near-death experience in a lightning storm while riding his horse one day. In the midst of his fear, he promised to dedicate his life to God if he survived. Being the deeply neurotic guy he was, Luther actually followed through on his promise and became an Augustinian monk. He spent much of his religious life fixated on the question of his eternal salvation (often when on the

---

3. *Farscape*, season 1, episode 20, "The Hidden Memory," directed by Ian Watson, written by Justin Monjo (2000; A&E Home Video, 2009), DVD.

toilet . . . look it up). I have many criticisms of Luther and his theology. That said, I find Luther's fear of hell and his anxiety over his salvation deeply relatable. Like many earnest young evangelicals, I spent much of my childhood and adolescence neurotically scared of ending up in hell and whether I believed sincerely enough when I accepted Jesus as my savior. I prayed the sinner's prayer at least twice a week throughout adolescence. If you spend much time at all in deconstruction spaces, it becomes quickly apparent that that is not a unique experience. I may not have *Ninety-five Theses* to nail to a cathedral door like Martin Luther, but having experienced such fear about salvation as a child has deeply impacted my work as a priest. Being drawn into ourselves and being obsessed with our eternal fate cannot be the life abundant Jesus declared in his ministry. I am driven to proclaim a Christianity that is not based around fear for our individual soul but is based in outward love, faith, and hope that we share with those around us.

Done Playing Defense 

Those in the broader progressive Christian or progressive clergy community online are no strangers to more conservative Christians demanding an accounting for our faith. I am often very hesitant to respond, which has sparked frustration and anger at a perceived lack of engagement with opposing ideas. The reality is, however, that progressive Christians and progressive clergy receive many questions and comments that are in no way offered in good faith or with any kind of humility. This is especially true for LGBTQIA+ Christians and clergy who are made to defend their very existence in the churches they serve so faithfully. Progressive Christians are regularly told that we are heretics and false teachers, that we are going to hell, or that we are sometimes literally Satan, all of which have been said to me personally in TikTok comments. It becomes overwhelming. Many of us are just done: done apologizing, done playing defense for who we are and for beliefs that are thoughtfully and reverently held. Conservative Christians who want to engage authentically should appreciate that distinction and not assume their way is the only way. I do not accept conservative evangelical Christianity as some kind of assumed default Christian position to which I am obligated to give answers. We should put our energy into proclaiming the gospel rather than trying to defend ourselves to a narrow segment of other Christians who have set their frameworks up as the standard for our shared faith.

Not a "Diet Catholic"

Robin Williams, may he rest in peace, is one of my top ten favorite Episcopalians. I will always and forever be a Robin Williams fangirl. He was a comedic genius, an underrated dramatic actor, and a deeply kind human being. I do, however, take issue with a popular bit of Williams's stand-up where he claimed that Episcopalians were Catholic lite: "same religion, half the guilt."[4] While the bit is undeniably funny, I do feel compelled to push back at this framing of Episcopalians. Episcopalians, and perhaps progressive Christians more broadly, have too often allowed ourselves to be defined and have even defined ourselves by what we are not rather than what we are. More conservative or dogmatic Christians will all too easily write us off with the dismissive "Oh, Episcopalians don't really believe anything anyway" or "You only have a church because

4. *Robin Williams: Live on Broadway*, directed by Marty Callner (2002; Sony, 2004), DVD.

Henry VIII wanted a divorce." We might even feed into that criticism when we default to positions, no matter how comedic, like having "ritual without guilt" or the recurring idea that "we're not like those other judgmental Christians!" The Episcopal Church has its own flaws. We do well to guard against becoming self-righteous about not being self-righteous. At the same time, we are far too hesitant to own the unique goodness in our spiritual and theological tradition. We are a deeply sacramental and traditional church, blending that richness of tradition with a commitment to justice and inclusion. We should not be defensive or apologetic of our expression of Christianity. We should embrace it and proclaim it!

Rejecting the Rapture 

Every kid raised in evangelical Christianity has a story about coming home to an empty house and for a split second being genuinely afraid they have been "left behind" in the rapture. Of all the theologies I have deconstructed, the rapture—the belief that at the end of time all those who are "saved" will be taken up into heaven while the rest of humanity is left to await tribulation under the Antichrist—is the most insidious. It is also one of the topics on which I receive the strongest response from others raised in persistent fear of the end-times. We are going to visit a couple of key points here, friends. First is that apocalyptic literature, of which the book of Revelation is a part, is not primarily about telling the future as it is about revealing the present. For example, Revelation is likely largely about the Roman Empire and not some future prediction. Second, and more importantly, the idea of the rapture with the "saved" getting pulled away and avoiding some coming tribulation did not exist in Christianity until its invention by Plymouth Brethren pastor John Nelson Darby and later popularization as a self-evident truth of Christianity in the 1920s in the Scofield Reference Bible. Once again, let us remember this key lesson: Christianity existed before modern American Protestants! Finally, I struggle with the idea of the rapture as pulling the "true" Christians away from suffering that will be endured by the rest of humanity. What is the heart of Christianity if not the story of the God who chose to share in solidarity with the fullness of our humanity—even to the point of suffering death?

Millennial Moments 

If there was one thing that defined growing up as a church kid in the 1990s, it was end-times hysteria. The world at large was stoking fears about Y2K and planes falling out of the sky. Meanwhile, many evangelical pastors were looking to the end of the millennium as a sign of Jesus's imminent return. There is a reason the Left Behind books rose to popularity around this time. It was against this background that I started college and began studying Old English literature. One of my formative moments in college was reading the *Sermo Lupi ad Anglos*, "The Sermon of the Wolf to the English People," written around the year 1000 by Wulfstan, archbishop of York.[5] Wulfstan could hold his own with the most turn-or-burn evangelical pastors. Looking to the turn of the year 1000, Wulfstan was warning of God's coming judgment. England had turned from following the teachings of Christ, and

5. Wulfstan, "Sermon of the Wulf to the English," in *The Anglo-Saxon World: An Anthology*, translated by Kevin Crossley-Holland (Oxford University Press, 1999), 294–300.

punishment was coming for their disobedience in the form of invading hordes of the Viking Antichrists! I can remember reading this text for the first time and being blown away, laughing at our all too human historical hubris. There really is nothing new under the sun.

Dismantling Lies and Owning Truth 

It feels insufficient to call M. L. Wang's *Blood Over Bright Haven* a statement on religious deconstruction. The dark academia novel explores numerous complex topics: colonial violence, patriarchy, and interwoven systems of oppression. At the core of the story, however, is the question of truth. What happens when the truth we believe grounds our lives is dismantled? Sciona is the first woman elevated to the status of high mage in the hierarchy of Tiran, a society built on the religious conviction of magic as a gift bestowed by God as a blessing on his chosen people. Through the course of her studies, Sciona discovers everything she had been taught is a lie built on profound evil.[6] On its own, such a revelation is a fairly common trope in much genre fiction. What sets Wang's work apart is how she explores what Sciona does in response. Wang does not hold back from the personal consequences such a discovery has upon Sciona, who must face the dismantling of everything she had ever been taught about truth and goodness. Wang asks us to wrestle with Sciona's earnest belief that if others just learn what she has discovered, they will immediately upend their culture and society as well. Spoiler alert: Sciona is very naive. As much as there is certainly a

6. M. L. Wang, *Blood Over Bright Haven* (Del Rey, 2024).

purely intellectual component to deconstruction, having one's entire worldview upended entails a dramatic personal cost as well. Those who have been through deconstruction know that the process can be brutal and often isolating. It is especially difficult to accept our participation in embracing theology that perpetuated harm against marginalized people. We must be prepared not just to change beliefs, but to dismantle how such beliefs shaped who we are and how we relate to the world. That is very hard, life-changing work.

Losing and Keeping Faith 

There is a kind of cliché about the conservative, earnest, religious kid going off to college and having their faith shattered by the liberal, secular, humanist academy. The *God's Not Dead* franchise has made big money off this. As it happened, the people I encountered in both college and grad school who most shook my faith were other Christians. My academic adviser attended my church and shared his irreverent Christian joy as we drank tea and translated *Beowulf* in his office. I had friends who were *gay* and Christian. I formed relationships with Catholics and even Christian Democrats. These relationships and frequent late-night dorm room conversations challenged many of my assumptions about the "right" way to be a Christian. Thanks to these friendships in my journey of deconstructing and reconstructing my faith, I never felt as if I was primarily moving away from something or trying to reject my evangelical background for its own sake. I was always moving toward an expression of faith modeled by my friends that felt more spiritually fulfilling. Quite honestly, I held on to my evangelical convictions for a long time. They just got worn down eventually by a faith that felt more compelling to me.

God annoyingly keeps revealing new depths of love and justice I'm constantly learning. Even now, more than ten years into life as a priest, I find my faith continuing to shift and change. "Deconstructing" is not a sign of weakness in our faith but of vitality. We are all works in progress and should not be afraid to let ourselves grow.

"The dogma is the drama" (Dorothy L. Sayers): Dealing with Doctrine

Ask a Better Question

When considering underrated figures in Christianity, Dorothy L. Sayers, a rough contemporary of C. S. Lewis, immediately comes to mind. While Lewis spent his life in the academy, Sayers (one of the first women to attend Oxford) spent several years working as an advertisement copywriter—a profession that gave her significant insight into economics and human nature. Indeed, many of her essays critique unfettered capitalism when such sentiments were still quite scandalous. Also unlike Lewis, who took the apologetics approach of asserting the self-evident rational truth of Christianity, Sayers asked a different question. Is it *worth* believing in Christianity in the first place? For Sayers, the "dogma" of Christianity was the "drama" of Christianity, "not beautiful phrases, nor comforting sentiments . . . nor the promise of something nice after death—but the terrifying assertion that the same God who made the world, lived in the world and passed through the grave and gate of death."[1] The story of the Christian faith might be accepted or rejected, but what was beyond question for Sayers was that it

1. Dorothy L. Sayers, "The Dogma Is the Drama," in *Letters to a Diminished Church: Passionate Arguments for the Relevance of Christian Doctrine* (W Publishing Group, 2004), 21.

was well worth believing. When asked about theology and church doctrine, we should always try to ground our answers not just as "is this *correct?*" but "does this *matter?*" As a side note, Lewis once wrote Sayers a letter asking her to join his campaign to ensure women could never be ordained to the priesthood in the Church of England—to which her response was simply "no." You do have to respect her for that.

Being as Communion

Christianity just might be the world's weirdest monotheistic religion. One God, three persons—what does that even mean? Most attempts to answer that question inevitably cross the line into heresy. For a fun overview of Trinitarian heresies, check out "St. Patrick's Bad Analogies" on the YouTube channel LutheranSatire, from which church nerds the world over quote "that's partialism, Patrick" in bad Irish accents every St. Patrick's Day.[2] However we articulate it, the doctrine of the Trinity serves as our best attempt to define God. Our language for that concept is inevitably insufficient to the divine mystery, but perhaps the most important truth to grasp with respect to the Trinity is that the nature of God's very being *is* the dynamic love that exists between the Father, Son, and the Holy Spirit. This is what we mean when we say that God's being is love. Orthodox theologian John Zizioulas expresses this dynamic by noting that we are called to take on God's "way of being," which is not about moral achievement but "is a way of *relationship* with the world, with other people and with God, an event of *communion.*"[3]

---

2. "St. Patrick's Bad Analogies," posted March 14, 2013, by LutheranSatire, YouTube, 3 min., 49 sec., https://www.youtube.com/watch?v=KQLfgaUoQCw.

3. John D. Zizioulas, *Being as Communion: Studies in Personhood and the Church* (St. Vladimir's Seminary Press, 1985), 15.

When we talk about ourselves being made in the image of God, that means we are beings created for communion and community. Does that make sense? Probably not. Nevertheless, wrestling with this mystery is core to the Christian faith. In the very essence of God's being, God is love. We who are created in that image are created to live into that reality of radical love of God and one another.

You Will [Not] Be Assimilated

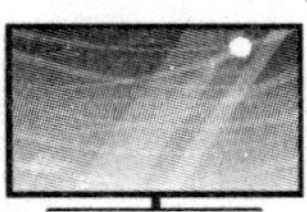

Are the Borg from *Star Trek* a good explanation for the Trinity? The answer is: not at all. For context, the Borg is a hive-like alien entity that shares a collective consciousness and defeats other races through the process of assimilation. Why is this a bad model for understanding the Trinity? Because the whole point and mystery of the Trinity is that within the unity of the godhead is the distinction of the persons of the Father, the Son, and the Holy Spirit. That is precisely what makes the Trinity so hard to define. If our humanity is made in the image of God, the nature of the Trinity has implications for who we are and how we understand our salvation. In progressive Christian spaces, we often push against the idea of hyperindividualized personal salvation, especially those who have come from more evangelical traditions. In doing so, we can come up with this idea of hypercollectivized salvation in which God is more concerned with humanity as an entity than with particular people. The beauty of Christianity lies in the tension of those two extremes. We are saved and redeemed as a human race by the God who chose to share our humanity. In our reconciliation with the perfect love of God and our neighbor, the distinctiveness of our personhood remains. We are not, in fact, assimilated.

Literal Resurrection

While I have deconstructed and reconstructed much about Christianity, there are two bedrocks of faith I hold with deep conviction: God became human in the person Jesus of Nazareth, and that person, Jesus, rose from the dead. In the Christian story, God literally enters human time and space. We refer to this as the Incarnation, or as the Gospel of John states: "The Word became flesh and dwelt among us." The Incarnation has profound implications for how we understand God and our identities as human creatures whose flesh God chose to share. It has ramifications for what it means for us to honor the dignity of every human being, particularly the most vulnerable and marginalized. Submitting to death on the cross is God's ultimate act of solidarity with humanity in our weakness. God willingly surrendered to death at the hands of the most powerful empire in the world, but the story does not stop with that seeming defeat. In the resurrection, God conquers the power of sin and death. The promise of the resurrection is that the world does not have to be the way we think it is. Jesus has conquered sin and death and everything that is wrong and unjust in our world. The challenge for us is to live into that mystery in true, grounded joy.

Breaking Cycles

Yet another assumption I have to combat far too often is that I don't take sin seriously. I do, in fact, believe in both sin and the need for repentance. It's not hard to look at the world with its brokenness and appreciate the reality of sin. While I believe in the concept of original sin, I do not accept original sin as a stain on each individual soul passed down from the seed of Adam. Like most things in the Western church, this idea is largely traceable to St. Augustine of Hippo and would later feed into the Calvinist theology of "total depravity," where humans are fundamentally incapable of goodness outside of the grace of God. The Eastern Orthodox church, however, teaches the notion of generational sin. According to this view, sin is learned from our ancestors, rather than being literally passed down through generations. The human race into which we are born fails in many ways to live into the fullness of God's love. Much like generational cycles of abuse get passed on within families, generational cycles of sin are learned and replicated as a consequence of our shared humanity. Christ, as the perfect embodiment of God's love, shows us a better way. Reframing the conception of original sin has significant implications for salvation as well. Is salvation about avoiding a punishment, or about restoring us to full communion with God?

Missing the Mark 

What is sin, exactly? In addition to the idea of "generational sin," the Orthodox tradition also helpfully frames sin as "missing the mark" of God's perfect love. What if part of the reason we have such a hard time pinning down a definition of sin is that we are often trying to provide a positive definition to something that does not have positive existence? We talk about Christian life in terms of the "thou shalt *not*" behaviors we are trying to avoid, instead of considering the practices we are meant to follow. Rather than identifying specific rules and lists of dos and don'ts, perhaps it is more valuable to consider the virtues we are meant to cultivate. Paul called these virtues the fruits of the spirit, such as love, joy, peace, and patience. Sin is less about "doing bad things" and more about our inevitable failure to live fully into those virtues. If sin does not have a positive existence, then what is it? The clearest answer is a lack of love. One verse that can change our thoughts about sin is 1 Peter 4:8 (NIV), "love each other deeply, because love covers over a multitude of sins." There's also the classic 1 John 4:7–8, "Let us love one another, because love is from God; everyone who loves is born of God and knows God. Whoever does not love does not know God." As he was preparing for the crucifixion, the final commandment that Jesus gave his disciples in John 13:34–35 is to love one another so much that our love will be the mark by which people recognize that we are followers of Christ. If sin is a lack of love, then embracing love is embracing faithfulness.

The Virgin Birth

Hot take, but the doctrine of Jesus's Virgin Birth is actually pretty feminist. Let's consider how God the Father worked through a human woman alone to bring about the incarnation of Jesus. Men had nothing to do with it. There are admittedly good reasons to be critical of Christian doctrine of the Virgin Birth. It has been harmful to women in promoting an absolutely impossible ideal of womanhood—women should be both sexually pure and mothers at the same time. Women can never win! Sometimes, however, our well-meaning attempts to bring our faith more in line with progressive values can have unintended consequences. In seeking to downplay the emphasis on Mary's virginity or wanting to give Mary sexual agency and autonomy, we end up with something that is a lot less radical than what the "orthodox" Christian faith just *is* at its core. When we look at the genealogy of Jesus, it is women who stand out: Rahab, Tamar, and Ruth. Given that these stories were written in a highly patriarchal context, such inclusions in Jesus's lineage are worth noting. Seen in this light, God's calling of Mary as the God-bearer, or (in Greek) the *theotokos*, without the involvement of a man, takes on a whole different level of feminism. Properly understood, the doctrine of the Virgin Birth can tell us quite a lot about those through whom God chooses to work.

Prayer: It's Not About Us

Cædmon, credited by the Venerable Bede in his eighth-century *Ecclesiastical History* as the first named English poet, might also be lauded as the patron saint of introverts. We meet Cædmon at a gathering where guests are taking turns telling stories. Rather than face his turn when it comes up, Cædmon runs away. Surely, anyone with social anxiety who has sat in a prayer circle waiting for the moment to come when you are expected to present a perfectly crafted spontaneous prayer can relate to Cædmon here. Unlike Cædmon, we may not escape to a barn where an angel awaits to divinely inspire with words for the song of creation. We can, however, disappear into the ancient prayers of the Church. Formalized liturgies are sometimes accused of being "vain repetitions as the heathens do" (Matthew 6:7, NKJV), little more than mindless regurgitations of the same words over and over. Perhaps, though, there is freedom in being released from the expectation of performance. Worship is not about perfectly executing a display of devotion to God, which then becomes subject to scrutiny and judgment from others. Liturgical prayer is about our shared act of praying together collectively—both people gathered in one physical space and those gathered across barriers of geography and time. There is profound humility in such unity, but there is also a gift in being released from ensuring our individual expression of worship conforms to others' expectations. We live in a world that places a high value on individuality and authenticity. That is good in many ways! Sometimes, however, we need permission to not focus so pointedly on ourselves. Prayer—whatever that looks like for us—seems the perfect time for that redirected focus.

Labels Are Hard 

I love being a part of the progressive Christian community, especially among the friends and colleagues I have encountered online. I do, however, resist the "progressive" label to some extent. I absolutely support the full, unapologetic inclusion of LGBTQIA+ folks within the life of the Church. As a female priest, I obviously advocate for women in leadership. I believe the gospel compels us in no uncertain terms to seek justice and liberation for people of marginalized identities and those who experience oppression. There is certainly a progressive impulse in those values. The work of inclusion and justice is ongoing. I am here for challenging traditions and institutions that do harm. At my core, though, I am a fairly conservative person. I don't really believe in progress just for the sake of progress. I think that it is important for us to have a kind of intellectual humility with respect to the wisdom of the past. The medievalist in me will always mourn parts of the medieval worldview—like the enchantment with creation and the ability to hold mystery, paradox, and wonder—that are neglected in our enlightened modern worldview. Maybe we should resist putting ourselves or others in boxes with neat labels and focus on the work of living into God's call to love one another in increasingly inclusive ways.

"Read, mark, learn, and inwardly digest" (Book of Common Prayer): Pondering the Scriptures

Is the Bible Sacred?

A few years back, I was talking to an evangelical pastor colleague about organizing a local clergy Bible study. He told me that he would be happy to meet with me, but he could not study the Bible with me because he saw the Bible as "sacred" and I did not. I genuinely did not know how to respond, so I just walked away, gobsmacked at his assumption. I absolutely see the Bible as sacred, but perhaps we need to define our terms. When I use the term "sacred," I am talking about something that points beyond itself to the divine. When we talk about sacred space—whether we are talking about a place of worship like a church, or a particularly beautiful place in the mountains—we are talking about a place that, for some mysterious reason, connects us to the presence of God. When

---

"Blessed Lord, who caused all holy Scriptures to me written for our learning: Grant us so to hear them, read, mark, learn, and inwardly digest them, that we may embrace and ever hold fast the blessed hope of everlasting life," Collect for Proper 28, Book of Common Prayer, 236.

I say that I believe the set of writings comprising the Bible is sacred, I mean that it points beyond itself to a revelation of God. In my ordination vows, I stated that I believe "the holy scriptures of the Old and New Testaments to be the word of God and to contain all things necessary to salvation." I stand by that. We need not believe that the Bible must be infallible to be held as sacred. Perhaps the power of a sacred text is that despite complicated history and inevitable human error, the scriptures still do contain the Word of God for us. The Bible does still give us the wisdom we need in order to live into the promise and hope of our salvation. When we become too focused on the Bible as an end in itself, however, it ceases to be sacred and becomes idolatrous.

You Don't Have to Take My Word for It! 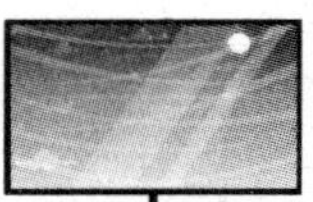

In 2013, the Toronto Comicon hosted a panel with LeVar Burton, mainly about his role in *Star Trek: The Next Generation*. At one point, though, a member of the audience brought up *Reading Rainbow*, which prompted Burton to lead a sing-along of the theme song with everyone in the room. The response of the audience to that song speaks to the impact of a show like *Reading Rainbow* that taught a generation about love of reading. Every episode would feature kids sharing about their favorite books, ending with the line "but you don't have to take *my* word for it," encouraging viewers to check out the book in question for themselves. The act of reading and engaging with stories is necessarily participatory. Reading is always an act of interpretation. This is one of the greatest critiques of biblical literalists—the people who claim the meaning of the Bible is self-evidently clear and allows for no interpretation. That cannot be true of any text. It is certainly not true for a text as varied as the Bible, written by multiple authors in a wide range of genres and historical circumstances. The most honest way any of us can approach the Bible is with self-awareness of our own biases and interpretive frameworks. Most importantly, we should view the Bible as an invitation for us to join in the larger story of God's love for God's people. But don't take my word for it!

Sheathing the Sword

My first great act of rebellion in my evangelical upbringing was dropping out of Bible Drill, also called "Sword Drills." Bible Drill was a big deal in Southern Baptist culture. Each year, kids and youth would have a selection of Bible verses and "key passages" to memorize. We would participate in highly regulated competitions that progressed from church to regional to state level. Around fourth or fifth grade, I simply refused to participate anymore. Even as a kid, I suppose my stubbornness made me resistant to the idea of rote memorization without a greater purpose, though some friends who also came from evangelical Christianity will talk about their gratitude for the scriptural foundation they gained from the tradition, even if they ultimately moved away from it. Learning to recite John 3:16 according to the proper King James wording did not help me have a sense of what it truly means that God loved the world and sent his son to die for us. Being able to find the book of Philemon in under ten seconds did not teach me how to wrestle with the reality of slavery in the biblical text. Being able to recite the minor prophets in order certainly did not open my eyes to the profound witness of social justice in the Hebrew scriptures. It is not enough to know the content of the Bible if we never learn how to interpret that content. It took moving into a tradition looked down on by other Christians as having a "low" view of scripture to appreciate the Bible not as a sword but as a comprehensive witness to God's love throughout human history.

Back to Basics

It may seem counterintuitive, but insisting on a purely literal reading of the Bible is quite a modern concept. Once more with feeling: Blame the Enlightenment! Did you know that the early church fathers had multiple frameworks for reading scripture? The literal/historical framework was only one of them. The others are often referred to as the typological (drawing allegorical connections, often between the Old and New Testaments), the moral (how scripture teaches us to act), and the anagogical (how scripture speaks to the future). It is absolutely true that the historical sense of scripture was the foundation of all other scriptural interpretations. As a consequence of the Enlightenment and its hyper-rational quest for certainty, however, both liberals and conservatives tend toward the *reduction* of scriptural interpretation to literal historical truth. Well-meaning academic projects, such as the liberal "Jesus Seminar" of the 1980s, set out to verify everything Jesus said and did historically, while placing less emphasis on the purpose of Jesus's teachings. We do the Bible a disservice when we try to look at it through only one lens, especially when that lens is not one the text itself claims to uphold. The Bible is riddled with factual contradictions, even in its accounting of an event as central as Jesus's resurrection! We don't have to go back to a precritical lens of scriptural interpretation, but we do need to study the manuscript history of scriptural texts and dig deeply into their historical contexts. We must also remember literal or factual truth is not the only, nor even the most important, meaning to draw from the Bible. How does the Bible call us to live? How does our interpretation of scripture draw us deeper into the love of God and our neighbor? Whatever frameworks we employ, they should help us answer those questions.

Rachel's Bible Hour 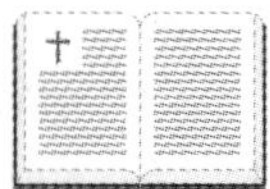

I used to read the Bible in order to keep myself from being bored in church as a kid. That sounds very pious, but in fact, my undiagnosed ADHD brain was reading all the stories in the Bible the Sunday school teachers did not want us to know. I actually got in trouble on a youth mission trip for holding "Rachel's Bible Hour" at meals, where I would share about Lot and his daughters or the last few chapters in the book of Judges. Apparently summarizing the literal content of the Bible constituted mocking God's word. While much has changed in my faith, it seems I am still criticized for simply reading the Bible. I used to get in trouble for sharing salacious stories from scripture. Now I get in trouble from a certain subset of more conservative Christians for reading the words of Jesus. It's rather ironic that I don't even advocate for a purely literal reading of the Bible, and yet I do take Jesus at his word when he says that the greatest commandment is the love of God and love of our neighbor. I listen to Matthew 25, where Jesus determines entry to heaven based on how we have treated the poor, imprisoned, and hungry. I take to heart Mary's words in her song of praise on learning she will give birth to the Messiah: "He has filled the hungry with good things, and sent the rich away empty" (Luke 1:53). I will not pretend my own reading or interpretation of scripture is perfect. What I do not accept is that progressive Christians don't take the Bible seriously or just choose to ignore it entirely due to how we read it.

The Rules of the Game 

Any type of interpersonal engagement without clarity about our rules of engagement is inevitably going to end badly. For example, the most popular show on the niche comedy streaming network Dropout is *Game Changer*. As the title might suggest, the game itself changes every episode, and the participants have no idea of the rules before the show begins. This has led to some amazing hijinks, like when frequent Dropout cast member Brennan Lee Mulligan realized the only rule was that he alone could never win any points, and his subsequent rant about it. As much as *Game Changer* is a silly show based on a ridiculous premise, there is a deeper point to be made from it. We cannot meaningfully play a game if we are not clear on the rules. This is arguably the root of a lot of the frustration between conservative and liberal Christians trying to have meaningful conversations about the Bible. We are playing by different interpretive rules! Progressive Christians don't accept that the Bible is without error and must be read literally. Evangelicals don't get to establish the default rules for biblical interpretation just because they often set themselves up to be "biblical" Christians, as if anyone who disagrees with their framework is not. We may never agree on what the rules are, but the only way we can have meaningful engagement across different biblical interpretations is at least to be aware of the rules by which we are each playing. Those of us who hold more liberal or progressive frameworks for scriptural interpretation should also be reminded that we do not have to play by fundamentalist or literalist rules.

Fake Paul

Who is Fake Paul? Why is Fake Paul responsible for many (if not all) the issues a lot of people have with Real Paul? It's time to learn the word *Pseudepigrapha*, a fancy term for anonymous texts written with the assumed voice and authority of various biblical patriarchs and prophets. Essentially, pseudepigrapha or "fake naming" is the practice of taking on the name, identity, and style of someone in order to lend authority and credibility to one's own writing. It's important to take off our modern authorial hats and recognize that this was not a nefarious practice. Pseudepigrapha was widespread into the early Middle Ages. Essentially, the way scholars determine whether something is "legitimate" Paul or "pseudo" Paul is based on writing style, syntax, grammar, and potential dating of texts and manuscripts. The scholarly consensus is that Ephesians and the Pastoral Epistles (Titus or 1 and 2 Timothy) were not legitimately written by Paul. Some contention exists over the authorship of Colossians, 2 Thessalonians, or 2 Corinthians. Significantly, most of where we see ideas like Paul telling women to be silent in church come from the Pastoral Epistle, aka Fake Paul. We can recognize that those "pseudo Paul" epistles were adopted into the Christian canon. They have been held as authoritative by the Church, and of course, being "fake Paul" does not negate that history entirely. When these texts have been used, for example, to deny the ministry of women and to assert the infallibility of scripture as a whole, we must be willing to wrestle honestly with their authorship. We do not have to deny the messy human history in the composition of the Bible to believe God still speaks to us through the scriptures.

Tackling the Old Testament 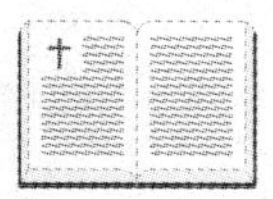

Comedian and late-night host Taylor Tomlinson is excellent, especially her bits drawn from experience growing up in church. Exvangelical church kids love religious trauma–based comedy! However, there is one joke in particular that never sits well. Joking about her thought that "God must hate me" when she hit puberty, she quips: "That's a joke. God doesn't hate anyone. Anymore. But have you read the Old Testament?"[1] Tomlinson goes on to joke about the God of the Old Testament smiting unbelievers like a spiteful Taylor Swift lyric. The bit is obviously funny, but it falls into a trap that many people raised in Christian spaces, including progressive Christians and ex-Christians who left conservative churches, fall into. We accept it on face value that the New Testament reflects a warm, cuddly Jesus preaching love and forgiveness, while the Old Testament God is at best a tyrannical bully in the sky. It is important for us to realize this is actually a pretty anti-Semitic attitude. It suggests that our Jewish siblings, whose Hebrew scriptures are very close, if not identical, to the Christian Old Testament, follow a backward religion of a vengeful God. It is important for us to sit with both the harsh stories in the New Testament, such as Ananias and Sapphira in Acts (5:1–11), as well as stories of God's abundant love in the Old Testament, such as the love story in the book of Ruth or the drama of deliverance from slavery in Exodus. From the very beginning, God's love pushes human boundaries.

Love Is Our Lens

How *does* a progressive Christian read the Bible with all of its complexity? What does it mean to hold it as any kind of authority, or as divinely inspired? How do we avoid our own biases? The best any of us can do is be honest about the biases and agenda we bring to the text. If there is one rule to use as

1. Taylor Tomlinson, *Look at You*, Netflix, 2022, https://www.netflix.com/watch/81471774.

an interpretive framework for scripture, it is Jesus's own words: "By this everyone will know that you are my disciples, if you have love for one another" (John 13:35). We must always ask: Does our reading of scripture produce the fruit of love? The doctrine of hell does not produce good fruit. It produces religious trauma and tells us God works through punitive rather than redemptive justice. Readings of scripture that do not allow for the full affirmation of LGBTQIA+ identities do not produce the work of love. Such readings drive people to despair and even potentially self-harm. We cannot read scripture in the abstract. We must always judge our readings of scripture by the "fruit" it produces. The arc of scripture in all its complexity and contradiction is, quite simply put, the story of the God who loves us, refuses to give up on us, and calls us to share that love with one another.

"I believe. Help my unbelief" (Mark 9:24): Tackling the Tough Questions

Faith and Doubt

There is a touching moment in the Gospel of Mark in which a father brings his demon-possessed son to Jesus, begging Jesus for healing. Jesus tells him: "If you can believe, all things are possible," to which the father responds, "Lord, I believe. Help my unbelief." What constitutes belief? Can belief and unbelief coexist? Faith is not something that we have or don't have. Faith does not exist in opposition to doubt, but in a dynamic relationship with doubt. The father's desperation compels him to believe Jesus must be able to cure his son. But he does not *know.* The best he can do is ask Jesus to help his disbelief. In response, Jesus does not condemn him or judge him. Jesus accepts the father's faith in the imperfect state that it is offered. One of the powerful aspects of the Episcopal tradition, for example, is that we recognize faith is a communal reality. On the days when we struggle with doubts, as happens even for clergy, we trust that the community and the tradition are able to hold the faith for us. Faith is not a burden we are each expected to bear perfectly on our own. We can and should rely on one another to help us in our inevitably imperfect belief. Are there times we can recall shouldering the weight of faith for someone else?

Whose Christianity Matters? 

It has become commonplace online to condemn Christianity outright as being a religion of oppression and injustice. I always want to respond by asking: What Christianity do you mean? Is it the Christianity that inspired Archbishop Desmond Tutu to fight the system of apartheid that oppressed the black population in South Africa? Or the queer theology that allows many LGBTQIA+ Christians to boldly claim their belovedness before God? Christianity has many evils for which we must answer, especially given the ways in which we have often aligned ourselves with political power at the expense of the vulnerable. At the same time, Christianity is a religion through which many people facing suffering or oppression have found strength. Christianity is *both* the religion of the Jim Crow South and a major source of inspiration for the Civil Rights Movement. We must be careful of seeing Christianity as one homogenous thing, especially when it means accepting Christianity as primarily defined by its most privileged adherents. We do that, and very often, it is precisely the most marginalized voices within Christianity that end up getting erased. White supremacy and patriarchy are insidious forces, even when we are seeking to condemn them.

Embracing Proximity 

In the process of reconstructing my Christianity, one of the things I needed to accept was finding comfort with a faith that does not have easy answers for everything. The top of that list is the question of human suffering. I do not fault anyone who chooses to walk away from religion in general or Christianity specifically because there is not any easy answer to this question. What I can say for myself is that in Christianity, I find the image of God who does not remain distant from our pain and suffering. In much of liberation theology, we hear the voices of marginalized people who find in the cross the image of the God who stands in deep solidarity with their pain and their oppression. As people called to live following the example of that God, we are called to live in solidarity with the pain of the world around us and particularly in solidarity with marginalized and oppressed people. That is powerful. It means that no matter what forces of oppression or injustice seem to be winning in the world at different times, God is always on the side of the oppressed. No one has the power to change that fact. This notion of God's solidarity with human suffering comes with a clear call to how we are to live in relationship with one another. Civil rights attorney Bryan Stevenson articulates this as the call to embrace "proximity" with the needs of the world, which he manifests in his activism for those wrongly convicted on death row.[1] How do we resist the temptation to preserve our own comfort by stepping back from the suffering we see around us? What might embracing proximity look like?

"Forgiveness. Can You Imagine?"[2] 

In the musical phenomenon *Hamilton*, Eliza accepts Hamilton back after his affair with Maria Reynolds and the loss of their

1. Bryan Stevenson, *Just Mercy: A Story of Justice and Redemption* (Spiegel & Grau, 2015), 17–18.

2. Lin-Manuel Miranda and Jeremy McCarter, *Hamilton: The Revolution: Being the Complete Libretto of the Broadway Musical with a True Account of its Creation,*

son, who died to defend his father's honor. The chorus expresses simply: "Forgiveness. Can you imagine?" Forgiveness has to be both the best and the worst teaching in Christianity. In Matthew 18:21–35, Jesus answers Peter's question of whether we should forgive as much as seven times, with the commandment given to forgive, not just seven times, but *seventy times seven times*. Jesus follows this teaching with a parable condemning a man who receives a great forgiveness of debt himself and cannot extend such grace to another who owes him far less. The grace of forgiveness is undeniably beautiful. Nevertheless, the Church needs to be honest about how that burden of forgiveness has often been unduly placed on the marginalized and victims of abuse. When forgiveness is weaponized to become a burden upon those already oppressed, it is no longer good news. If we look just a few verses back, it is clear that an attitude of forgiveness does not always lead to reconciliation with those who don't own the wrong they have done. We forget that forgiveness is meant to be a promise of freedom. We are not bound by the pain and the resentment of whatever trauma is in our past. Forgiveness is ultimately the work of God in whom we put our hope. Can we cultivate the faith to imagine such forgiveness?

Choosing Life

Pregnancy and childbirth are no joke. After the birth of my son, I noticed certain unresolved symptoms, but I was assured by the doctor's office that everything was fine. Everything was definitely *not* fine. I demanded an in-office appointment, where

---

and Concise Remarks on Hip-Hop, the Power of Stories, and the New America (Hachette, 2016), 254.

they discovered retained placenta fragments and scheduled me for immediate surgery. As the doctor was telling my husband the procedure was completed, I started bleeding out in the OR. I lost two liters of blood, and my bleeding only stopped because another doctor was scrubbed and ready to go in. Had I hemorrhaged at home, I would almost certainly be dead. As it was, I had to be readmitted to the hospital twice to get my blood levels back to normal. I have also, like so many others, experienced an early miscarriage. While I would never tell someone else how to feel about pregnancy or loss, I cannot pretend to view that lost pregnancy with the same moral weight as my two living children. I am radically pro-choice, not in spite of my Christian faith, but because of it. We choose life by ensuring anyone who finds themselves pregnant has adequate healthcare and resources to give birth and care for their child. We choose life by recognizing the disparity in material health outcomes for black women. We choose life by recognizing terminations of pregnancies in the second or third trimester are often the result of tragic situations where the child is desperately wanted. The parents deserve compassion, not condemnation. Every pregnancy is different. Every pregnancy poses different joys, challenges, risks, and sorrows. If we do in fact care about the complexity of life created by God, we must say that no legal framework can possibly capture those nuances.

Spiritual Scars

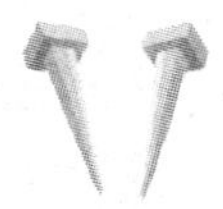

Religious trauma is very real and all too often dismissed. Many of the people who frequent "religious deconstruction" communities share similar stories. I have heard too many people confess to being told the issues in churches are not systemic, they just had "bad experiences." Maybe their faith was not strong enough and they were not *really* Christians to begin with. Responses like this compound the realities of church hurt, as it becomes clear that friends and loved ones will default to defensive protection of the religious traditions and institutions rather than sitting with the pain being expressed. I am often asked how I got over my own religious trauma. I am a priest after all. I have reconstructed my faith, and I love the teachings of Jesus. I must be "healed," right? The honest answer is no, I am not magically over my religious trauma. I doubt I ever will be entirely. I struggle with generalized anxiety disorder that likely developed from the persistent fear in childhood and adolescence that I was not actually saved and might at any moment die and be cast into eternal torture. That's heavy stuff for a kid! I find it helpful to think of spiritual scars like any other scar. The immediate hurt does heal, but the mark remains on our souls. I recognize the irony of continuing to work in a religious tradition that, while different in many ways from the one I left, is far from perfect. With God's help, I seek to walk faithfully with others still in the process of owning the reality of their pain, assuring them they are not alone. Perhaps, if you hold such scars, hearing a priest confess to similar experiences might help you feel less alone as well.

I Don't Have All the Answers! 

I will let you in on my not-so-secret interfaith pet peeve: interfaith dialogue that reduces religions in all their diversity to watered-down liberal Christianity. During a hospital chaplaincy internship in seminary, I was introduced to a "Gold Rule" poster that shows the same teaching (Jesus's famous "Golden Rule") as it manifests in various religious traditions. Obviously, there is nothing wrong with encouraging us to consider the similarities that appear across different religions.

It is vital to see our commonalities! That said, I have often seen this image and others like it used to flatten the very real differences that exist between faith groups. This happens most insidiously among well-meaning progressive Christians who unintentionally end up presenting various religious teachings as little more than different expressions of Christian theology. As a college chaplain, I am deeply involved in interfaith work, which is both a blessing and a challenge. I love learning from Jewish, Muslim, Buddhist, Hindu, Pagan, and countless other communities about their faith and their traditions—even when their beliefs challenge my own. Embracing the wonder and mystery of God means letting go of the need to reconcile our beliefs with one another. I believe at the core of my being that God is definitively revealed to us in the person of Jesus Christ. I also believe that God is big enough and mysterious enough not to be exhaustively contained in one story. Are those beliefs contradictory? Maybe. But I trust God to be able to work it out.

Self-Reflection

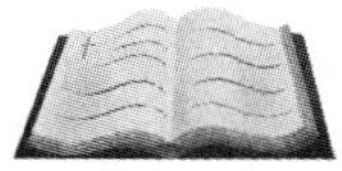

In the summer of 2020, The Episcopal Church made headlines in the midst of the Black Lives Matter demonstrations in Washington, DC. After President Trump ordered peaceful protestors to be cleared out of Lafayette Square Park, he infamously had himself photographed at the nearby St. John's Episcopal Church holding an upside-down Bible. Episcopalians nationwide were rightly up in arms about one of our churches being used for this photo op for Christian nationalism. The then Presiding Bishop Michael Curry condemned the president's use of a church building and the Holy Bible for blatant partisan purposes. This took place in a time of deep hurt and pain in our country. I am far from the first person to name this, but the question that had to be asked is: Why was there an Episcopal church right there on the steps of the White House in the first place? As an Episcopal priest, I wrestle with the power and privilege my church has historically held in this country. I am troubled by prayer appointed for July 4 in the Book of Common Prayer, which describes America as an explicitly Christian-founded nation: "Lord God Almighty, in whose Name the founders of this country won liberty for themselves and for us, and lit the torch of freedom for nations then unborn."[3] Are we as a church too comfortable with our own subtle versions of Christian nationalism? The Episcopal Church has been called the "church of presidents," and the National Cathedral is often the venue for significant state funerals. What aspects of our historical privilege might we need to sacrifice to live into our stated values? These questions are far from unique to Episcopalians. These sorts of questions are ones many historic institutions must face, such as other historic churches as well as colleges and universities. If we honestly wish to dismantle systems of injustice, we must be willing to address our participation in them.

But What If We Are Wrong? 

One of the biggest challenges when deconstructing is the question of fear. What if we're wrong? If we are deconstructing from a religious worldview that told us the consequences for false belief would be literal eternal torture, the stakes for being right or wrong are impossibly high. We need to name that high-control religion can be spiritually and emotionally abusive. Like other types of abuse, it leaves psychological, if

3. Book of Common Prayer, 242.

not physical, scars. We should be gentle with ourselves, given how hard it can be to overcome that fear. As we work through that trauma, however, it is worth shifting our thinking from whether we are right or wrong to whether our beliefs make us more compassionate and loving. We all have to ask ourselves, what makes us better in this world? What, to use religious language, bears good fruit in my life and in the world around me? What in our understanding of God challenges us to make the world better for other people? Speaking from my own experience, my religious upbringing did not equip me to answer those questions. I was taught to be fixated on my own righteousness and the sincerity of my own faith. To the degree I was taught to love others, it was for the sake of "evangelism." My faith did not make me compassionate, let alone concerned with liberation or justice more broadly. I came to realize that even if the faith of my childhood was right all along, I would not want to worship that version of God. That realization has brought me peace. Deconstruction inevitably involves a leap of faith. At some point, we all have to decide what we are willing to risk being wrong about. Especially as we see increasing numbers of Christians excusing and embracing white Christian nationalism, I will say it as I have said before: If the worldview I was brought up in is true, I am proud to be wrong.

HOPE

"All shall be well"
(Julian of Norwich, *Revelations of Divine Love*)

For over twenty years, I have kept a photo in my bedroom of friends gathered around our college dorm room celebrating my roommate's birthday. On the surface, it looks like any other photo of smiling college students. What makes this picture significant is that it was taken on September 10, 2001. The next day we would go to our Tuesday morning classes hearing reports of a terrorist attack in New York. We would then go to lunch, where we gathered for hours around the TV in the dining hall watching footage of the planes hitting the Twin Towers. Soon, we would be thrown into a new reality of the War on Terror and the Patriot Act. As the years have passed, the world seems to be unraveling more and more. We live under the looming threat of climate catastrophe, the rise of white supremacy, and a resurgence

---

Julian of Norwich, *Revelations of Divine Love* (1901; Project Guttenberg, October 23, 2024), chap. 27, https://www.gutenberg.org/files/52958/52958-h/52958-h.htm.

of fascism—not to mention the fact that the COVID virus is here to stay. It is a running joke among members of my millennial generation that we are tired of living through history-defining events. The world so often feels like a dumpster fire, and yet I cannot let go of my determination to *hope*.

Hope is a tricky thing. There is a danger in allowing hope to become something naive that can lull us into passivity. We are right to reject religious calls for hope that fall back on the idea that "God's got this!" or that what truly matters is some eternal kingdom of God and we need not be concerned with the troubles of this world. Instead, we hold onto hope as a bulwark against the temptation to despair. Hope pushes against the mindset that tells us our world is so broken that there is no capacity for it to change. Such nihilism becomes a different excuse for inaction, especially on critical issues such as climate change or racial injustice. I find myself coming back again and again to the words of the fourteenth-century writer Julian of Norwich in her *Revelations of Divine Love*: "All shall be well, all shall be well, and all manner of things shall be well." Julian's words are not an indifferent dismissal of the suffering endured in this world—after all, she watched her community be ravaged by the plague. Instead, her words are a profound message of *hope* that the love of God is stronger than any evil brought about in this life.

This section explores the different dimensions of that radical hope. What does it mean to persist in hope when the world feels so profoundly *hopeless*? How might our perspective on judgment change if we view it within the framework of God's restoration, not as God's punishment of us? Most importantly, I invite us to embrace hope for the reconciliation of all people into God's redemptive love. If we believe our hope of salvation is not just about a prize in the afterlife but transformation of the world *now*, how does that transform the way we live?

"Wait and see. The world is not always cruel" (T. Kingfisher, *Nettle & Bone*): Hope in a Hopeless World

Knitted Socks and Mended Hearts

While it is always challenging to identify one favorite author, if forced to make a choice, it would have to be Ursula Vernon, known by her pen name T. Kingfisher.[1] I especially love her Saint of Steel, a series of romance novels centered on a group of Paladins, a class of holy characters in much generic fantasy, who are left traumatized by the death of their god. It does not help that said Paladins are prone to berserk fits of rage, now without divine protection. Kingfisher has many talents, but she specializes in broken Paladins. Steven, the hero of the first novel *Paladin's Grace*, notably copes with his trauma by therapeutically knitting socks. Kingfisher's brilliance lies in her ability to bring about a romantically satisfying ending without suggesting love solves all their problems. Steven finds love with a perfumer named Grace, but neither he nor his Paladin brethren are suddenly healed by true love. Steven continues to live with his cohort, where they care for one another, and he

1. T. Kingfisher, *Nettle & Bone* (Tor, 2022), 206.

spends his days sitting in Grace's workroom knitting socks. Kingfisher deftly embraces the "happily ever after" of the romance genre while allowing that happy ending to be nuanced. We can be "happy" and still work toward healing. All of us are, to some degree or other, a little bit broken. The movement of hope is the work of walking together, maybe knitting one another socks.

Carousel of (No) Progress 

There is something particularly ironic about getting stuck in the Carousel of Progress at Walt Disney World. There are only so many times one can listen to the attraction's theme song "There's a Great Big Beautiful Tomorrow"[2] on repeat before you start pondering what "progress" this carousel is actually celebrating. Dating from the 1964 World's Fair, the "carousel" is a revolving theater that rotates through scenes of an animatronic family demonstrating technological advances of the twentieth century. For all that the story celebrates "progress," it is hard to miss how little the family or characters themselves change as they cycle through the decades. Even in the final futuristic vignette, they remain a white, heteronormative, middle-class family. It's actually quite a conservative, even regressive, view of the world. Walt Disney might have been a visionary in many ways, but vision was lacking here. The hope expressed in something like the Carousel of Progress is both misplaced and too small. It's not enough to put our hope in technology to save us from climate disaster, war,

2. Richard M. and Robert B. Sherman, "There's a Great Big Beautiful Tomorrow (Carousel of Progress)," Walt Disney Music Company, 2025.

or fascism if we are not able to envision the deeper work of transforming our relationships with one another. Much like the Carousel itself, which circles on endless repetitions of the same story, we can become trapped in the same cycles of history when we do not allow ourselves to hope beyond what seems possible. May we always have a greater hope!

Planting Onions 

In one of her memoirs, Madeleine L'Engle talks about living and raising children in the midst of a fraught period in the Cold War. She famously wrote: "Planting onions that spring was an act of faith in the future, for I was very fearful for our planet."[3] Her reflection is reminiscent of a story in Luke 13:69 about a landowner whose fig tree is not bearing fruit. The owner of the tree wants to give up and tear it down, but his gardener responds: "No, put mulch around it, prune it, care for it. Give it another season to grow." The story is a reminder to us that even when we are ready to give up on this world that seems to bear no fruit of love or justice, God is not done with us. We are called to persist in hope. Both the story of the fig tree and L'Engle's anecdote about planting onions furthermore remind us that hope is manifested in action. With regards to the fig tree, the farmer does not suggest just sitting by and idly waiting for it to produce fruit. Rather, he encouraged tending to the tree. Similarly, L'Engle's account of planting onions speaks to an *active choice* to nurture crops she might not see grow to fruition. Hope compels us to plant our

3. Madeleine L'Engle, *And It Was Good: Reflections on Beginnings*, The Genesis Trilogy (Waterbrook Press, 2001), 12.

metaphorical onions in faith, trusting that God is not yet done with us or with this broken world. What does it mean to persist in *active* hope?

Sunrise on the Reaping

> *"And that's part of our trouble. Thinking things are inevitable. Not believing change is possible."*
> *"I guess. But I really can't imagine the sun not rising tomorrow. . . ."*
> *"Can you imagine it rising on a world without a reaping?"*[4]

This exchange between teenage lovers Lenore Dove and Haymitch Abernathy summarizes the heart of Suzanne Collins's *Sunrise on the Reaping.* Set twenty-four years before the main Hunger Games series, in which we see a bitter and broken Haymitch, *Sunrise on the Reaping* tells the story of Haymitch as the eventual victor in the fiftieth Games. His conversation with Lenore takes place the day before he finds himself cast into the Games. Lenore is a Covy, a group of people known for their eccentric, nonconformist relationship to the world. In contrast to Haymitch's resignation to the inevitability of violence and injustice, Lenore questions such assumptions. Must the sun rise every day—must the sun rise the morning of the reaping—just because it has every day in the past? What changes in the world do we resign ourselves to accept as impossible because it is too hard to imagine something different? *Sunrise on the Reaping* ends with a seeming victory for the status quo. Haymitch wins the games, but everyone he loves, including Lenore, is murdered by the capitol as punishment

4. Suzanne Collins, *Sunrise on the Reaping* (Scholastic Press, 2025), 10–11.

for his attempts at rebellion. Despite such a dire ending, the prequel also introduces us to the characters who work for decades to bring about the successful rebellion that we see come to fruition in the main Hunger Games trilogy. Over the course of the series, we readers know the sun *will* one day stop rising on the reaping for the Games. Hope challenges us to see beyond what the world tells us is possible. The work of hope is long, but it is worth pursuing.

The Taste of Strawberries 

One of the most heartrending moments in *The Return of the King* occurs when Frodo becomes so overwhelmed by the burden of the ring he has been bearing that he collapses in despair on Mount Doom. This is one moment where Peter Jackson's 2003 film amplifies the poignancy of the novel. Ever Frodo's stalwart companion, Samwise Gamgee tries to remind Frodo of the joys remaining in the world, like strawberries in springtime. Sam asks, "Do you remember the taste of strawberries?" To this, Frodo can only declare: "I can't recall the taste of food, or the sound of water, or the touch of grass."[5] In writing Frodo's despair, Tolkien was drawing on his lived experiences in the trenches of World War One. A bedrock of his faith is that even in the depths of such despair, we must hold a persistent glimmer of hope. Sam, whom we all know to be the real hero of Tolkien's epic, recognizes what Frodo has come to in his despair. In a moment of triumph, Sam carries Frodo to the top of Mount Doom with the powerful words: "I can't carry [the Ring] for you, but I can carry you

5. *The Lord of the Rings: The Return of the King*, directed by Peter Jackson (2003; Warner Brothers, 2004), DVD.

and it together!"[6] What might it mean for us to live as Sam in a world that seems determined to beat us down? The words of Luke's gospel call us not to let our hearts be "weighed down with dissipation and drunkenness and the worries of this life" (Luke 21:34). Unlike despair, which may allow us to stagnate in resignation, hope compels us to make this broken world better. How do we recall ourselves to hope? How can we commit to carrying one another in faith? Even as our reality disappoints us, we live into hope by holding on to a vision of what we want the world to be.

Look Forward, Not Back 

Octavia E. Butler's 1993 book *Parable of the Sower* is almost a little bit *too* prophetic in its depiction of the 2020s.[7] Butler crafts a vision of an American society beginning to crumble into the realities of climate change and rampant inequality. The main character, Lauren, lives in what was once a gated community in Los Angeles. Those in her immediate neighborhood struggle, but not nearly to the degree as those immediately outside their walls. Butler invites her readers to consider where we place our hope in a world that is falling apart. Many of the people in Lauren's community, especially among the older generations, long for what they no longer have. Their hope is in a world and way of life that is gone. They desire the times when they enjoyed comfort and security. In contrast, our protagonist Lauren sees potential for change, renewal, and ultimately community. While Butler's narrative will find resolution in new worlds beyond the limits of the earth, the

6. J. R. R. Tolkien, *The Return of the King* (Ballatine Books, 1993), 242.

7. Octavia E. Butler, *Parable of the Sower* (Grand Central Publishing, 2000).

framework of her story remains incredibly relatable for us over thirty years later. When the world is in upheaval, it is so tempting to place our hope backward instead of forward. How many of us, for example, jokingly longed for the "before-times" during the peak of the pandemic? As we live through significant uncertainty, we must be careful not to place our hope in a world that is dead and gone, especially when it wasn't entirely that great to begin with. Let's allow ourselves to be called into something new.

A Man of His Time 

For over a decade, my husband ran a YouTube channel where he gave advice and answered questions in the persona of the late 1930s cosmic horror writer Howard Phillips Lovecraft. Yes, this was an absurd premise, and yes, you can still find it at AskLovecraft.com. While his show was mostly a comedy, he did from time to time get drawn into more serious conversations, especially around Lovecraft's *very* overt racism. While I am not a fan of horror or Lovecraft myself, it was fascinating to watch these conversations play out, especially the way in which many of Lovecraft's readers would attempt to defend his indefensible prejudices. A line that came up again and again was "Well, Lovecraft was just a man of his time." My husband, who is not at all a Lovecraft apologist, would respond quite appropriately by saying that, yes, Lovecraft was a man of his time. He was also a man of Langston Hughes's time, and the writers of the Harlem Renaissance's time. When we dismiss problematic authors or public figures as just being "products of their time," we can end up accepting the privileged over the marginalized as the default voices of that time. We also forget that the only way we actually make change in the world is thanks to those who do not accept the injustices of their time as unchangeable.

The Devil's Lie 

The devil has many lies. Perhaps most insidious is the lie that the world is broken beyond saving. In his 2024 book *Devil's Contract: The History of the Faustian Bargain*, Ed Simon describes the story of Doctor Faustus, the German theologian who sells his soul to the devil, as "estimably modern, perhaps the first modern story."[8] Our modern lives seem defined by our willingness to make deals with the devil that lead us to sacrifice long-term goods for short-term gains. Our collective failure to disrupt our patterns of comfort and consumption in order to address the urgent threat of climate change is but the tip of the iceberg. The question we have to ask ourselves is whether the outcome of these devils' bargains are foregone conclusions. Elizabethan playwright Christopher Marlowe gives his version of Faust numerous opportunities to repent and turn away from his soul-bargain with the demon Mephistopheles.[9] Faust is repeatedly visited by an angel and a demon. The angel calls Faust to repentance, urging him that it is not too late to save his soul. The word over and over again from the demon is that such repentance is impossible. It is too late for him! This is the lie that leads to Faust's soul ending in hell. We might say Faust's damnation comes more from his lack of hope in the possibility of his salvation than in the devil's bargain itself. How often do we accept such lies about the state of the world or about ourselves? If we accept that we have no hope, the devil wins. More significantly, that lie spares us the harrowing work of repairing

---

8. Ed Simon, *Devil's Contract: The History of the Faustian Bargain* (Melville House, 2024), xxiv.

9. Christopher Marlow, *Doctor Faustus*, edited by David Scott Kastan and Matthew Hunter (Norton, 2024), Act 5, Scene 2.

the world or seeking the transformation that the work of justice and judgment would bring about in us. For Faust, surrendering to damnation is easier than being drawn into the work of hope. Let's make sure the same is not true for us.

But What If It Does? 

The phenomenal TV series *Derry Girls* (2018–2022) follows a group of adolescents living in Northern Ireland during the "troubles" of the 1990s and explores the innocence of youth against the backdrop of a harsh political climate. The show ends, appropriately, with the hope of the 1998 Good Friday Agreement between Irish and Catholic factions. In the final episode, the main character, Erin, struggles with how she will vote on the referendum, fearing that nothing can ever change the cycles of violence she has experienced in her young life. She confesses her uncertainty to her Grandpa Joe: "What if we do it and it was all for nothing? What if we vote yes and it doesn't even work?" To this, Grandpa Joe replies simply: "And what if it does?"[10] The series ends with Erin and her friends voting in favor of the referendum and walking into an unknown but hopeful future. Hope compels us to take risks. We do not always have the benefit of knowing with certainty how those risks will play out. Maybe our efforts will be in vain. Maybe we will not be able to fundamentally change the world. We know that history, thirty years on at least, has proven that the Good Friday Agreement did hold and provided a new future for a generation born in a historical place and time that

---

10. *Derry Girls,* season 3, episode 7, "The Agreement," directed by Michael Lennox, written by Lisa McGee, aired October 7, 2022, on Netflix, https://www.netflix.com/watch/81597614.

seemed without hope. Change can only happen because we listen to that voice in our hearts that, even amidst all the brokenness around us, compels us to ask: But *what if* it could be different? What if such a simple question could change our hope for the world?

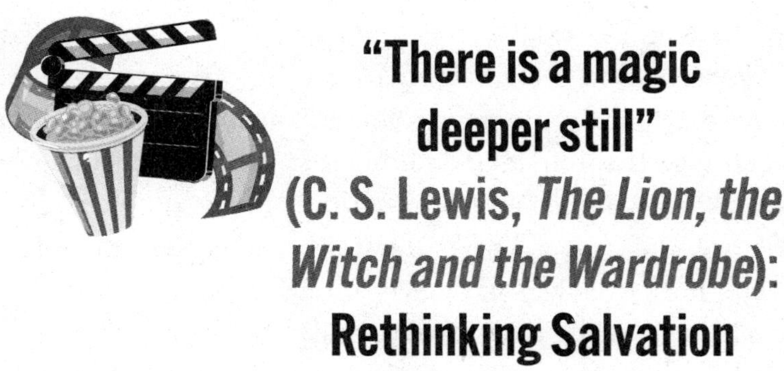

“There is a magic deeper still” (C. S. Lewis, *The Lion, the Witch and the Wardrobe*): Rethinking Salvation

Aslan’s Sacrifice

Even the most casual readers of *The Lion, the Witch and the Wardrobe* are aware that Aslan is a parallel to Jesus. We also know that Aslan’s self-offering in the place of Edmund provides a pretty straightforward parallel to Jesus’s sacrifice on the cross. It is worth noting, however, that Aslan’s sacrifice does not follow the understanding of Jesus’s crucifixion held as the default theology of the cross by many Western Protestant Christians, particularly evangelicals. Known as the theology of “penal substitution,” this conception of the cross asserts that, as sinners, humans are deserving of punishment from God. Jesus assumes this punishment by offering to die on the cross to satisfy God’s sense of righteousness. If we believe in Jesus and accept him in our hearts, we get the shiny gold medal of salvation (if we do not, a fiery future awaits). How does Aslan’s sacrifice play out for C. S. Lewis? In that story, the boy Edmund betrays his siblings to the White Witch, who then claims Edmund’s life as forfeit to her under the rules established at the founding of Narnia. Aslan gives his life for Edmund’s—dying, rising again, and saving all of Narnia according to the "deeper magic."[1] Yes, on the surface this sounds like penal substitution. But *Aslan* is not demanding Edmund's life as some justification of sin owed to himself. It is in fact the White Queen herself who demands Edmund's life. Salvation comes when Aslan willingly gives himself over to the queen and so confounds her power, breaks the stone table, and destroys the queen's hold over Narnia. Lewis is relying on a much older, more historic explanation of the crucifixion known as *Christus Victor.* The cross does not just take our punishment. It actually defeats Satan. Is that not truly Good News?

Blame Anselm!

How did the Church get to a place where it seems that the whole point of Christianity is that God had to brutally sacrifice his son so that we could be saved from eternal hellfire? Great question. The person you have to thank for that is Anselm, archbishop of Canterbury from 1093–1109. For the first thousand years of Christian history, the focus of Jesus's redemptive work on the cross was the idea of buying us back from the power of sin and death. Anselm's text *Cur Deus Homo* ("Why God Became Man") introduced the idea of *satisfaction* to the theology of the cross.[2] Anselm lays out the premise that our sin offends God's very medieval, Western notion of honor. The only thing that could avenge, or "satisfy," that sense of honor is a perfect sacrifice, hence Jesus as the God-man coming to pay satisfaction to God. This theology of "satisfaction" would eventually be developed by reformers like John Calvin

1. Lewis, *The Lion, the Witch and the Wardrobe*, 159.

2. Anselm of Canterbury, "Why God Became Man," *Anselm of Canterbury: The Major Works*, edited by Brian Davies and G. R. Evans (Oxford University Press, 1998), 260–356.

into the notion of "penal substitution" (Jesus takes the punishment for our sin demanded by God), the dominant theology of Western Protestants. Many contemporary Christians see penal substitution as the *only* theology of the cross—to the extent they write off as heretics anyone who questions it. Not only does this theology run the risk of making God seem very petty, it also dilutes the entire point of God becoming human to nothing more than the solution to a problem of God's own making. We do not have to accept as normative a framework for salvation that did not exist for the full first half of Christian tradition! How might our response to Jesus's sacrifice change if we truly embraced it as a gift, not a transaction we must accept in exchange for forgiveness?

The Joke's on Satan

When Stephen Colbert hosted Dua Lipa on his late-night show in February 2022, he and the singer entered into a vulnerable discussion of faith. In the course of their conversation, Colbert offered a poignant meditation on the resurrection. According to Colbert, who famously experienced the tragic death of his father and several siblings as a child, the central core of the Christian message is that "death is not defeat." We can look at every source of sadness or grief in this world as a sort of death. The ability to laugh at this grief is to not be defeated by it. Colbert's articulation of the resurrection as a kind of cosmic joke against the power of death is a pretty astute summary of how many early theologians understood the cross. Every year at Easter in my congregation, I read Saint John Chrysostom's Easter Homily, just referred to as *the* Easter sermon in the Orthodox tradition. While the whole homily is a beautiful articulation of the abundance and bounty of the Easter feast, the text ends with a summary of what some call the "mousetrap" theory of the cross—the idea that through his death, Jesus ensnared Satan in a trap:

> *Hell took a body, and discovered God.*
> *It took earth, and encountered Heaven.*
> *It took what it saw, and was overcome by what it did not see.*
>
> *O death, where is thy sting?*
> *O Hell, where is thy victory?*[3]

Far from being abstract or obsolete, these lines touch on the reversal at the very heart of Christian hope: that what the world tells us constitutes power and privilege is no match for self-giving, sacrificial love. The cross is God's last laugh at the devil.

No, but I Can Lose! 

The final battle between the titular hero and Dormammu in *Doctor Strange* (2016) has a fascinating theological undercurrent. Facing the inability to beat the "big bad," Doctor Strange traps himself in a time loop where he is defeated again and again by his adversary.

> *"You will spend eternity dying!"*
> *"Yes, but everyone on Earth will live. . . ."*
> *"You will never win."*
> *"No. But I can lose. Again. And again. And again. Forever.*
> *That makes you my prisoner."*[4]

---

3. John Chrysostom, "The Easter Sermon," accessed November 23, 2025, https://anglicansonline.org/special/Easter/chrysostom_easter.html.

4. *Doctor Strange*, directed by Scott Derrickson (2016; Marvel, 2017), DVD.

Scott Derrickson, who directed *Doctor Strange*, is a self-proclaimed Catholic filmmaker. His depiction of Doctor Strange confounding the power of evil through his willing defeat is a wonderful example of the *Christus Victor* model of the atonement. Christ's sacrifice was not a payment to Satan to buy us deliverance, as some critics have claimed. It was not some sacrifice to God to appease God's righteousness or wrath. The crucifixion is God staring down evil, sin, hell, and all that separates us from divine love, saying, "Do your worst," and utterly confounding the power of hell. Our salvation truly comes down to Jesus staring at Satan and saying, "I cannot win. But I can lose." This is the paradox at the heart of Christianity. The way of life comes through what looks like defeat. It might look like the cross gives victory to Satan. Rather, through the reality of the cross, Christ definitively upends the power of sin and death.

Are You Saved? 

We should talk more about C. S. Lewis's lesser known and weirdly whimsical friend: Catholic writer Charles Williams. At one point in Williams's *The Place of the Lion*, the main character, Mr. Richardson, is chasing down the Platonic forms that have entered the world and happens upon a small-town prayer meeting. A woman comes out of the church and asks him if he is "saved." Mr. Richardson reflects later that though the woman's question was kindly meant, "she reduced indescribable complexities of experience to an epigram."[5] Such a simplistic framing of salvation is often connected to verses

5. Charles Williams, *The Place of the Lion* (Regent College Publishing, 2003), 167.

like John 3:16: "For God so loved the world that he gave his only Son, so that everyone who believes in him may not perish but may have eternal life." It is ironic that this verse of scripture has been used to reduce the Christian experience to a formula: "salvation" in exchange for belief in Christ. In the context, Jesus is speaking about how the movement of God in wind and spirit cannot be reduced to human understanding. Being "born again" spiritually is not as simple as the physical process of being born. In *The Place of the Lion*, our protagonist does not reject the question of his salvation, but his answer allows for a less reductive framing: "I believe salvation is for all who will have it . . . and I will have it by the only possible means."[6] Maybe the means of our "salvation" is living into the mystery of God's love and seeking to manifest that love in our lives.

The Very Good Gospel 

A major issue specifically in predominantly white churches is the emphasis on "getting saved" as a question of whether or not we get to heaven when we die. I hope, in my reflections up to this point, I have pushed against such a narrow view of salvation. By no means do I want to discount the promises of eternal life, but I also believe the Western church has focused on individual salvation to the detriment of salvation as a communal reality. I credit *The Very Good Gospel: How Everything Wrong Can Be Made Right* by Lisa Sharon Harper with pushing me to embrace what salvation means for humanity as a whole, not just individual people. Inspired by a trip to King Center in Atlanta, Harper reflects that the Good News of an individualistic

6. Williams, *The Place of the Lion*, 165.

gospel "doesn't feel good enough."[7] Harper explores salvation from the framework of restoring "peace" or "shalom" across multiple spheres of relationship: racial reconciliation, environmental justice, and gender equity, to name a few. The ultimate goal of our faith isn't just the "salvation" of our individual souls. The goal of our faith is a life of redemptive love. We bear witness to such love in our relationships with one another and in our pursuit of radical justice for all people. According to this framework, salvation involves far more than receiving a blank slate of forgiveness for our personal sins and a "get out of hell free" card. Instead, salvation calls us to embrace the profound hope that God is working to bring about the redemption of our world that can seem so irreparably broken. We may not see the fulfillment of salvation on this side of eternity, but placing our hope not in the fate of our eternal individual souls but in the restoration of universal *shalom* should dramatically change how we live in our messy, broken world. If we hope for a world in which all people are reconciled in perfect love of God and one another, the way we live our lives should reflect that.

The Cross and the Lynching Tree 

As we push against the hyperindividualized notion of salvation in Western Protestantism, we must discuss the work of James Cone, the father of black liberation theology. Cone's 2011 book, *The Cross and the Lynching Tree*, builds on his foundation of black liberation theology to explore the cross as God's ultimate act of radical solidarity with the marginalized. Cone draws an

7. Lisa Sharon Harper, *The Very Good Gospel: How Everything Wrong Can Be Made Right* (Waterbrook Press, 2016), 2.

explicit connection between the image of Christ on the cross and the black and brown bodies brutalized in American history. Ultimately, in the cross, Cone sees God's promise of overturning all systems of oppression, radically and definitively. Cone writes that doubt is not an antithesis to faith. Doubt keeps faith from being sure of itself, but in the context of our faith, doubt does not get the last word. The last word is "faith giving rise to hope."[8] As we have discussed, hope is not naive optimism. Hope is not certain. Our hope is specifically rooted in the work of Jesus and the reminder that God has acted definitively in choosing to dwell with our humanity. In the work of the cross and submitting to suffering even to the point of death, God has sided definitively with the most marginalized and the most oppressed. The core of that faith allows us to persevere in hope, working for a world of justice and liberation. What might it look like for predominantly white churches that want to embrace the vision of Martin Luther King Jr.'s "Beloved Community" to sit with the work of repentance and dismantling our historic complicity within the systems of oppression and white supremacy in our nation? Cone both challenges us to see and invites us to join that vision of liberation.

Beyond Perfection 

Multi–Olympic gold medalist Simone Biles is widely considered the greatest female gymnast of all time. I am far from a gymnastics expert, but even to my untrained eye, her performances stretch the limits of what seems humanly possible. Every time I watch one of her routines, though, I am struck by how often she will step out of bounds on a tumbling

8. James H. Cone, *The Cross and the Lynching Tree* (Orbis Books, 2011), 106.

pass. Despite this, Biles still wins consistently because her difficulty is so out of this world in comparison to her competition. She can afford the deduction. Simone Biles is awesome. Simone Biles is *phenomenal* in her greatness. Simone Biles is also not perfect. She is in fact *extraordinary*, which is so much better than perfect. We are not meant to aim for static perfection. As we wrestle with our various frameworks for what salvation is, let's remember that salvation most certainly is not a matter of obtaining some kind of individual moral perfection. It is true that Jesus tells us to "be perfect, therefore, as our heavenly Father is perfect" (Matthew 5:48). We might ask, though, what is the nature of God's perfection? Surely it's more than some static moral perfection. We have discussed God's being as the relation of love that exists within the persons of Trinity. God simply *is* perfect love beyond our comprehension. When we consider the nature of our salvation, that image of love should be our model and where we place our hope.

Is the "Good News" Good? 

Given that I have been referred to as "literally Satan" by online trolls, my detractors will no doubt find it fitting that I once spent a summer touring Eastern Europe as Satan. For context, I was playing the villain character in an evangelical drama as part of a mission trip to save Hungary and Romania from (checks notes) Roman Catholicism and Eastern Orthodoxy. We would perform our drama, narrated in the local language, then we would go out into the unsuspecting crowds with actual note cards with the evangelical plan of salvation written in parallel English and Romanian/Hungarian. If someone decided they did want to accept Jesus, we would bring them to a translator, lead them through the sinner's prayer, and mark them down as a victory for the Holy Spirit.

Many of the people we "won" for Christ were Romani or others living on the streets. I will never forget performing in the same neighborhoods multiple days in a row, often seeing the same people who got "saved" the day before continuing to beg for their livelihoods on the side of the street. Did we talk to them again or try to do anything to improve their quality of life? No. That summer, it began to really occur to me that if we believe the life and ministry of Jesus has meaning, it must impact our lives and our world in some tangible way. Jesus fed the multitudes. He healed the sick. Jesus cared not just for the souls of those he encountered but for their material reality as well. It is easy for me to roll my eyes at the absurdity of American teenagers doing pantomime on the streets of Budapest, thinking we were doing something for the kingdom of God. All the same, "liberal" churches can often prioritize preserving our institutions and traditions over witnessing to the love of God in our communities. Let's demand more from the gospel and how we live into it!

"God Is Bigger Than the Boogie Man" (*VeggieTales*): Justice and Judgment

Wisdom from Bob and Larry

If you ask most disaffected '90s exvangelicals to name one thing from church with which they still have positive association, they will probably say *VeggieTales*. Who wouldn't love a series of stories and songs about God's love told by CGI vegetables? In an early episode, Junior Asparagus struggles to go to sleep after watching a monster movie, and Bob the Tomato and Larry the Cucumber comfort him with the song "God Is Bigger Than the Boogie Man."[1] God is in fact watching out for us, and no monster—real or pretend—is tougher than God. While this song may be meant as reassurance for children afraid of imaginary monsters, there is a deeper truth to it as well. God is, in fact, bigger than all those evil forces of the world that (justifiably!) seem so scary to us. As the world gets more frightening, I put more and more hope in the radical love of God. In addition to her famous declaration that *all shall be well*, Lady Julian of Norwich had a famous vision of all human sin and saw that it was but the size of a hazelnut in

---

1. *VeggieTales*, "Where's God When I'm S-Scared," directed by Phil Vischer (1993; Sony Wonder, 2004), DVD.

the hand of God. How might our commitment to hope change if we could truly believe that? How would our sense of God's judgment, not to mention our conception of hell, change if we believed that there is no force of injustice, oppression, or violence that is stronger than the reconciling love of God?

Defeating Dragons

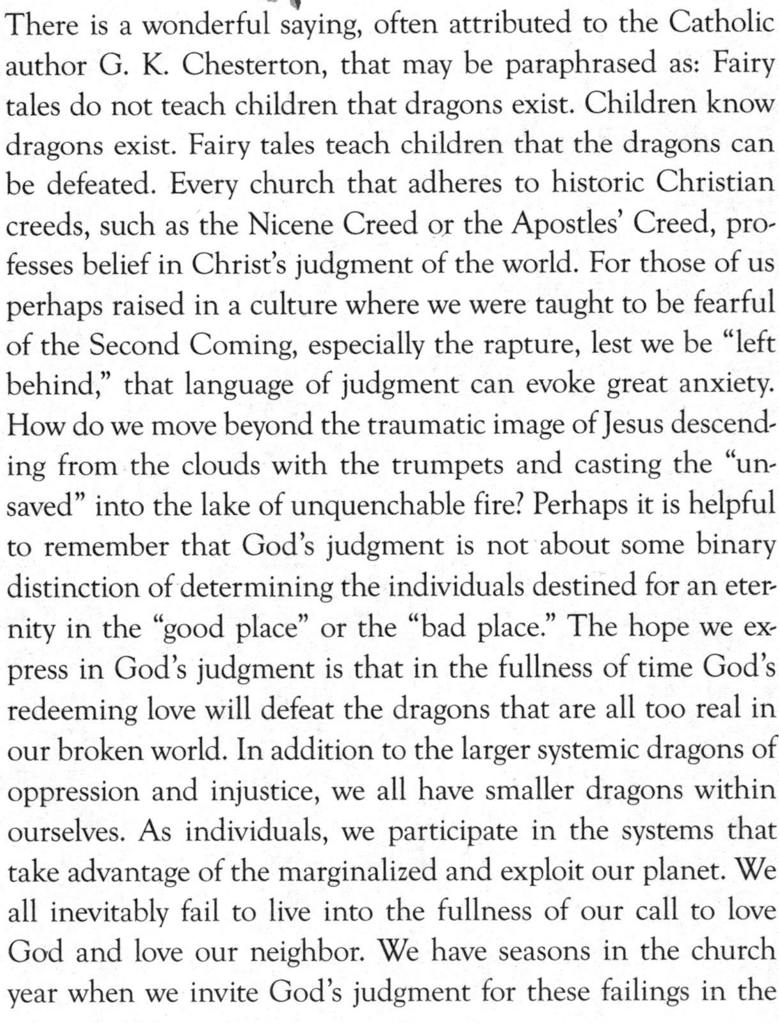

There is a wonderful saying, often attributed to the Catholic author G. K. Chesterton, that may be paraphrased as: Fairy tales do not teach children that dragons exist. Children know dragons exist. Fairy tales teach children that the dragons can be defeated. Every church that adheres to historic Christian creeds, such as the Nicene Creed or the Apostles' Creed, professes belief in Christ's judgment of the world. For those of us perhaps raised in a culture where we were taught to be fearful of the Second Coming, especially the rapture, lest we be "left behind," that language of judgment can evoke great anxiety. How do we move beyond the traumatic image of Jesus descending from the clouds with the trumpets and casting the "unsaved" into the lake of unquenchable fire? Perhaps it is helpful to remember that God's judgment is not about some binary distinction of determining the individuals destined for an eternity in the "good place" or the "bad place." The hope we express in God's judgment is that in the fullness of time God's redeeming love will defeat the dragons that are all too real in our broken world. In addition to the larger systemic dragons of oppression and injustice, we all have smaller dragons within ourselves. As individuals, we participate in the systems that take advantage of the marginalized and exploit our planet. We all inevitably fail to live into the fullness of our call to love God and love our neighbor. We have seasons in the church year when we invite God's judgment for these failings in the world and in ourselves. Our invocation of God's judgment is not about fear for our souls. It is about the hope that God's love is stronger than the dragons born of human evils. As we look ahead to that judgment, we also ask ourselves: How can we strive to live into the fullness of our hope even now?

What Can We Change?

In 2023, Ray Minniecon, an Aboriginal pastor with roots in the Kabikabi and Gurang-Gurang tribes of Queensland, gave a talk at a gathering of the Colleges and Universities of the Anglican Communion in Melbourne, Australia. He addressed the urgency of reparations for indigenous communities in Australia. To do the work of reparation and reconciliation requires forgiveness, which he went on to define with a phrase that stuck with me: "Forgiveness is letting go of the hope of a different past."[2] By no means did Pastor Ray suggest that his people forget the injustices of colonialism. He was brutally honest about his experiences and those of his community. Elsewhere, he has said pointedly, "Healing is a meaningless word for Aboriginal people because we possess a wound that cannot be healed."[3] At the same time, Pastor Ray was clear that if we want to have any hope of building a future based on transformative justice and true liberation for all people, we must accept the realities of the past for what they are. We all—both oppressors and oppressed—must reckon with the past honestly and openly. The evils of the past cannot be undone. While we may not be able to change history, we do get to

2. Ray Minniecon, Keynote Address, Triennial Gathering of the Colleges and Universities of the Anglican Communion, Melbourn, Australia, July 7, 2023.

3. Ray Minniecon, *The Forgiveness Project*, accessed November 22, 2025, https://www.theforgivenessproject.com/stories-library/ray-minniecon/.

decide how we move forward. We can advocate for racial reparations in response to the historic disenfranchisement of African Americans. We can embrace the Land Back movement being led by Native American communities. Living into the hope that cycles of injustice and oppression can be broken may give us the courage to face the painful realities of our past. Only then can we demand a better future.

Tell a Different Story 

Some of the most humbling and transformative work I have been a part of in my ministry has happened through my engagement with Palestinian Christians. I have to express my admiration for my colleagues Rev. Canon Leyla King, Rev. Lauren Grubaugh Thomas, and Rev. Nicole Janelle, with whom I have worked to found Palestinian Anglicans and Clergy Allies (PACA). PACA is a grass-roots organization aimed at educating the wider church regarding the experiences of Palestinians, especially Palestinian Christians. My colleagues within this network, and the Palestinians with whom we partner, witness to me daily about the power of rejecting narratives that serve to support the existing power structures of colonialism and empire. If there is a group in the world who would be justified in abandoning hope, it would be the Palestinians. Instead, the Palestinian pastors with whom I have engaged continue to challenge the Church in the West to reject false binaries, such as the belief that in order to stand in solidarity with the Jewish people, we must ignore the cries of Palestinians. They call us to embrace hope rooted in abundance, not scarcity. I find myself coming back again and again to words that I once read from Mitri Raheb, a Lutheran pastor and theologian in the West Bank: "Dismantling Empire starts with believing there is something more potent than the

Empire."[4] The work of justice in dismantling oppression, moreover, is rooted in a hope of God's judgment that is more potent than punishment or retribution. My Palestinian friends and colleagues articulate very clear calls for justice regarding the oppression they have experienced at the hands of Israel for three generations. Such justice, however, is rooted in the hope of reparation and liberation for both oppressor and oppressed. God's judgment is not a zero-sum equation.

The Medium Place 

As we continue unpacking the nature of God's judgment, let's chat about purgatory, a particularly misunderstood concept in the Christian tradition. We have been conditioned to think of purgatory as a kind of "medium place" in the afterlife, as opposed to the good place (heaven) and the bad place (hell). Mindy St. Claire, the medium place resident in the TV series *The Good Place*, gets to enjoy her favorite beer, but it is always warm. Her jukebox plays her favorite songs, but only bad covers.[5] It is easy to see why many Christians write off this idea of purgatory as unbiblical. In the image of purgatory, the arms of Christ are stretched wide on the cross. Evangelical Protestants are taught that purgatory is a way to limit the saving grace of God. In truth, when properly understood, purgatory expands God's grace. Purgatory is not just a place where medium

---

4. Mitri Raheb, "Jesus Responds to Empire," in *Normalize or Resist?: Palestinian Christians Respond to Oppression*, edited by Andrew F. Bush (Bethlehem Bible College Publishing, 2024), 44.

5. *The Good Place*, season 1, episode 12, "Mindy St. Claire," directed by Dean Holland, written by Megan Amram and Jen Statsky, originally aired January 19, 2017, on NBC.

people wait out an unending limbo of mediocrity because they fit neither in the good place or the bad place. However we may conceive of it, purgatory is where we are literally purified by God's redeeming judgment. Reconciliation with God is not just about getting a clear slate from sin, but it is about actually being transformed into the image of God's perfect love. Interestingly, *The Good Place* does in its final episodes develop something like the idea of purgatory. In the afterlife, everyone goes through a process for as long as needed to learn what they must in order to make it to the "good place." Even Mindy St. Claire leaves her "medium place" and submits to this truer form of purgatory. It's a concept of the afterlife that certainly merits our hope.

The Snare of Self-Righteousness 

Hope in God's judgment applies not just to the world around us, but to the brokenness that inevitably exists within all of us. If there is one character in popular culture who represents what it is to be "lawful evil," it is Inspector Javert from *Les Misérables*. He spends the play hunting down our protagonist Jean Valjean, whom he knows as prisoner 24601, for stealing bread to feed his sister and her child. We follow Valjean's story from prisoner to a gracious town mayor to a loving adoptive father. All the while, he is being hunted by the morally upright Javert, who will not stop until he brings Valjean to *his* idea of justice. Toward the end of the story, Valjean has the opportunity to kill Javert but instead lets the other man go. Javert's whole worldview, defined by rigid lines of right and wrong/good and evil, crumbles under this act of mercy from the man he hunted. Unable to accept such grace, the inspector ultimately takes his own life. His story is a cautionary tale against righteousness that has no room for transformative or redemptive justice. In Javert's mind,

Valjean is a criminal who must be punished, no matter the circumstances that led to his choices or the harm that would be perpetuated by his imprisonment. Javert's commitment to punitive justice for its own sake seeks to achieve nothing beyond perpetuating his own ideas of right and wrong. His sense of justice does not look to make the world better. It does not seek healing where there is hurt. Such punitive justice can achieve nothing more than compounding harm upon harm. Javert's lens of punitive justice compels him not only to hold others to his rigid standards of righteousness but to impose such standards on himself as well.

Shedding Our Dragon Skin

There's a moment in *The Voyage of the Dawn Treader* when Aslan encounters Eustace on "Dragon Island." Eustace Clarence Scrubb, so unpleasant as to be almost deserving of his unfortunate name, has found himself on a high-sea adventure in Narnia with his cousins Edmund and Lucy. While exploring a mysterious island, Eustace falls asleep on a pile of dragon gold and wakes up to find that he himself has been transformed into a dragon. In his despair about never changing back into a human, he wanders off from the rest of the group, where he meets the lion Aslan, who, let us remember, is Jesus. Aslan pierces Eustace's skin with his claw, only to find another layer of dragon scales underneath. The process is repeated several times, until Eustace's new skin is finally revealed, at which point Aslan casts him into a pool of water in a clear symbol of baptism. Both the water on Eustace's skin and Aslan's claws piercing the dragon scales are painful, but they are necessary. Aslan does not just *forgive* Eustace for all of the ways he has been horrible, but he peels away the dragon scales, a symbol of his monstrous personality. As the story progresses, C. S. Lewis notes that while Eustace's "salvation" does not immediately transform his personality, it is more accurate to say "he had begun to be a different boy."[6] While he, and we ourselves, might still have a long way to go in terms of living into the image of God's perfect love, we have the hope that we can in fact be transformed. We are not stuck in our most monstrous moments.

Do a Little Good 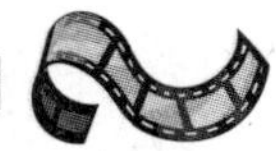

Is the movie *Spirited* that dropped on AppleTV in 2022 a retelling of, sequel to, or commentary on the original story of *A Christmas Carol*? All of the above? It's also a musical! Will Ferrell plays the ghost of Ebenezer Scrooge, who stages *A Christmas Carol*–style interventions during the holiday season, intended to get other less-than-saintly individuals to change their ways. We eventually realize that Scrooge has thrown himself into this work because he fears that he is "irredeemable" and that his Christmas-miracle transformation did not actually stick. What Scrooge must come to learn is that redemption is not a one-and-done event, but it is an ongoing process of renewal. It is undoubtedly tempting to put our hope in dramatic moments of instantaneous transformation. As the characters express in the final production number "Do a Little Good," the process of redeeming ourselves is not a straight line.[7] That is actually a good thing! Repentance is not something we have to get right one time. Repentance is the process of seeking again and again to move toward the fullness of God's presence in our lives and in the world and being transformed into the image of God's

---

6. C. S. Lewis, *The Voyage of the Dawn Treader* (Collier Books, 1970), 93.
7. *Spirited*, directed by Sean Anders (2022; Apple Studios, 2022), Apple TV+.

perfect love. Maybe if we genuinely grasp that, we can extend a little more grace both to ourselves and to one another when we start fearing any of us are "unredeemable."

Giving and Receiving Grace

I am not going to lie: It can be weird working as a chaplain at my undergraduate alma mater and pastoring the congregation I attended as a student. I have been here ten years at this point. I still find it surreal to see my former professors sitting in the pews when I preach! Suffice it to say, I am a very different person now than I was at the age of nineteen or twenty. I came to college as a very earnest evangelical Christian. My husband and I have been together pretty much since first-year orientation (big Lily and Marshall from *How I Met Your Mother* vibes), and we still laugh about how I was hesitant to date him because he was not "Christian enough." While I laugh at my younger self, some of the views I held as a teenager and young adult actually fill me with deep remorse and shame—particularly my attitudes toward LGBTQIA+ identities. It would have been so easy for people to give up on me back then. I hold deep gratitude for the friends who walked with me during the more insufferable stages of my life. I'm humbled by the community I serve that embraces me for who I am now, not who I was twenty-five years ago. There is nothing I can do to change things I have believed in the past or reverse the harm done by my beliefs and actions. I can make my work of repentance the commitment I have *now* to proclaim unapologetically the radical, inclusive love of God. My hope in the Good News is that we are all given the chance not just to be *forgiven*, but to actually move forward into the fullness of God's love. May we accept that hope for ourselves and live into the call to extend such grace to those around us.

"Hell no longer needs a keeper. . . . It needs a healer" (*Lucifer*): Hope Beyond Hell

Healing and Wholeness

I sometimes surprise people when they find out I am a priest who loves *Lucifer*, by which I mean not the literal devil, but the TV series that ran from 2016 to 2021.[1] The show features Lucifer, played with devilish charm by Tom Ellis, who has decided to take a break from lording over hell to live the high life as a nightclub owner in Los Angeles. Lucifer rebels against the status thrust on him as the "keeper" of hell, the one responsible for overseeing punishments imposed on those who find themselves condemned to hell's torments. As I discussed in the previous section, punishment is a brutal business. At the risk of overspoiling, the show ends with the realization that "hell no longer needs a keeper. . . . It needs a healer." Lucifer, having spent the series confronting his own literal and figurative demons, goes on to open his own therapy practice in hell, giving the damned a chance to move past being

1. *Lucifer*, season 6, episode 10, "Partners 'Til the End," directed by Sherwin Shilati, written by Joe Henderson and Ildy Modrovich, aired September 10, 2021, on Netflix, https://www.netflix.com/watch/81259971.

trapped in their own guilt. Yes, *Lucifer* is a sometimes-ridiculous procedural detective series. Still, I cannot overstate how much that simple shift in thinking about hell as a place of redemption resonates with my faith regarding the purpose of God's judgment. Once again, the gospel literally means *Good News.* What *good* comes from hell existing as a place of never-ending torture or from judgment that has no purpose beyond punishment? Embracing radical hope invites us to radically rethink the doctrine of hell.

Hell: What Is It Good For? 

> *"The God of eternal retribution and pure sovereignty proclaimed by so much of Christian tradition is not, and cannot possibly be, the God of self-outpouring love revealed in Christ." –David Bentley Hart*[2]

No belief I have expressed online has received as much backlash as my conviction that all people will ultimately be redeemed in the fullness of God's love. Please note, this is a far more nuanced hope than just believing "everyone becomes a Christian in the end." So many people across the theological spectrum have come to accept a hell of eternal torture as a necessary part of Christianity. I do not have words to adequately express how much I appreciate the absolutely uncompromising rejection of the doctrine of hell by Orthodox

2. David Bentley Hart, *That All Shall Be Saved: Heaven, Hell, and Universal Salvation* (Yale University Press, 2019), 90.

theologian David Bentley Hart. For Hart, rejecting hell is not just *possible* within Christian "orthodoxy" but necessary. Hart's deep reading of the Bible and interrogation of Christian tradition can basically be summed up in the following argument: Humans are finite, mortal creatures. No finite, mortal creature can commit sins great enough to justify *eternal* torture. Therefore, there can be no framework in which a God can *justly* condemn humans to eternal punishment. We may even take this a step further and remember that God's judgment is fundamentally *restorative*, not *punitive*. What *good* can actually be brought about by eternal torture from which may come no hope of redemption?

Two Can Play That Game! 

Let's talk about proof texting and "gotcha" Bible verses. Like every other woman with a platform online, I deal with no shortage of trolls. I am at least entertained by the people who call me things like "literally Satan," but I get rather annoyed with the commenters who will just drop a random Bible verse in my comments as if that's suddenly going to make me rethink my entire life and ministry. While 1 Timothy 2:12 ("I permit no woman to teach") is a frequent flyer, I get numerous comments refuting my belief in universal salvation, such as Matthew 25:46 (Jesus separating the sheep from goats and casting the goats into eternal "hell"). The fact is, the Bible is a frustrating collection of diverse texts, compiled by various authors with distinct agendas. I can very easily respond with gotcha verses of my own: 1 Corinthians 15:22 ("For as all die in Adam, so all will be made alive in Christ") or John 12:32 ("I, when I am lifted up from the earth, will draw all people to myself"). Somehow, the people who drop their proof texts in my comments never feel compelled to respond to mine. Ultimately, a battle of proof texts and gotcha passages doesn't really get us anywhere. The point is not to get into a war about proof texting, but to ask the bigger question of what the scope of scripture and tradition tells us about a God whose judgment is redemptive rather than punitive. Do we hope in a God of endless punishment or boundless grace?

Imagining Heaven 

Graduate school for medieval studies offers fun classes with titles like "Doomsday, Damnation, and the Devil: Antichrist in Anglo-Saxon England." One thing that class, and my general background in medieval literature, taught me is how much our Christian imagination of heaven is so impoverished. We have mountains of Christian literature describing the tortures of hell, and our imaginations seem to be captivated by it. People in college classrooms read Dante's *Inferno* much more consistently than they do *Paradiso*. I find it telling that the Left Behind series creates a charismatic villain in Nicolae Carpathia the Antichrist, while heaven is ruled over by a robotic, authoritarian Jesus. More popular conceptions of heaven paint saccharine images of cherubs on clouds playing harps. I do not claim to know what salvation will look like, though if I were forced to describe a physical place it would probably look a lot like the Shire in *The Hobbit*. All the same, I have to hope that the idea of being fully embraced in the love of God should inspire us to greater heights of imagination than the horrors of hell. If we can challenge ourselves to greater hope in our conception of heaven, how much might that change the ways we live out our calling to be witnesses of it in this present life? How might that improve our time on Earth?

Let Us Have Cake! 

When we were trying to finish our dissertations, my friend Alice and I developed a cunning reward system. We got points based on how early we got to the library or how quickly we finished certain tasks. When we reached a certain number of points, we would go out for fancy slices of cake at a nearby bakery. If either of us finished a chapter draft that meant automatic cake! We tallied our points jointly, a fact that Alice's then-boyfriend (now husband) Mike found humorously scandalous. A more motivating system should obviously have us competing against one another. Competition makes winners! What is the point of winning if someone else isn't losing? Now, obviously, Mike was being tongue-in-cheek and not actually bothered by our collaborative system. I have, however, encountered far too many people who are far too serious in their outrage at the idea of God's boundless grace—people who actually are scandalized at the idea of there not being a hell of eternal torture for the "unsaved." It is as if salvation is seen as a prize, one not worth having if everyone else gets it too. What does it mean for us to "win" heaven if there are no losers? It's worth noting that Jesus himself addresses these sentiments in the parable of the laborers (Matthew 20:1–16). All those who work in the vineyard receive the same payment, whether they worked one hour or the entire day. Heaven is neither cake nor a payment for service. It certainly is not a limited commodity. The fullness of reconciliation with God is not diminished by its abundance. How might our hope of heaven change if we embrace the idea of a salvation not as a status we attain, even if one freely given by God's grace, but as a reality we are invited to share?

All Means ALL

Over the past decade there has been a noticeable shift in a lot of Disney movies where the antagonist is not a monster but is instead a concept like self-doubt (*Moana*) or generational trauma (*Encanto*). Rather than the bad guy getting thrown off a roof, the story relies on a more nuanced resolution—Moana restores the Heart of Te Fiti and Abuela recognizes the cost of her unresolved grief on the rest of the Madrigal family. There are plenty of criticisms of the belief in universal salvation I reject, but one that is hard to dismiss is: "But what about Hitler?" I often hear claims that universalism emerges from some desire for an inoffensive, easy-to-digest version of Christianity that fails to acknowledge the reality of sin or evil. Universal salvation is a *hard* belief to hold precisely because all means all—including the villains of human history. That is scandalous. The hope in universal reconciliation pushes against our natural sense of justice. Quite honestly, I have seen plenty of commentaries on *Encanto* that struggle with Abuela's easy reconciliation with the rest of her family based on how much harm she inflicted. The hope of universal salvation, though, is really more about God than it is about us. Those of us who hold to universalism do not do so because we fail to take seriously the reality of human evil and the depth of violence we have inflicted on one another throughout our history. Rather, universalism is about the radical hope that God's love in the fullness of time will prove stronger than human evil, even as we wait for its fulfillment.

What About the Harm? 

Discussing the challenges of universal reconciliation is one thing when it comes to Disney villains; it is another thing when it comes to the villains of our own experiences. While writing this book in the summer of 2025, the world learned that James Dobson, founder of Focus on the Family and author of books *The Strong-Willed Child* and *Dare to Discipline*, had died at age eighty-nine. Not only was Dobson an advocate for parental "discipline" that far too often crossed the line to abuse, his work laid the groundwork for the rise of Christian nationalism in the American right (for more background on this I suggest Kristen Kobes Du Mez's *Jesus and John Wayne: How White Evangelicals Corrupted a Faith and Fractured a Nation*). Much "discourse" arose about how to respond, especially as many people who experienced abuse based on Dobson's teachings were accused of "celebrating" his death. As a former "strong-willed child" myself, I wrestled with what it meant to hope for the salvation of someone who had been responsible for so much individual and societal harm. The best I could come up with was to express my hope that Dobson is now fully in the presence of the radical love of God that he denied so many. My ultimate hope is that the fullness of God's refining love is stronger than Dobson's hate. I hope one day, even he will have the chance to atone for any harm he may have caused in life and be reconciled to such abundant love. In the meantime, we continue to proclaim God's love to those whom Dobson and his followers declared to be unlovable, particularly members of the LBGTQ+ community. Through such radical love for one another, we allow our present life to be shaped by that hope we long to see fulfilled.

Holding the Door Open 

We should never underestimate the impact of a simple invitation. When I was in grad school, I began attending an

Anglican church in downtown Toronto near the university campus with my friends. I am sure we made quite the sight, coming to church laden with our backpacks, sitting in a back pew, then sneaking off for lunch at Tim Hortons and work in the Pontifical Institute of Mediaeval Studies library as soon as mass was over. Each week, the rector Father Mark would see us at the door and cheerfully invite us to coffee hour: "Are you going to stay this week?" Each week, we politely declined. At some point, we started volunteering with their food ministry. Eventually, I was drawn into being an acolyte, and then the church more or less took over my life. I found myself confirmed in the Anglican tradition and then rapidly finishing my PhD dissertation so I could start seminary. Father Mark was and still is a deeply important pastoral mentor. To this day, I recall his gentle but persistent invitation to us after mass every Sunday. He never made us feel guilty and never pressured us to become more engaged than we were comfortable with. But the invitation was always there. This is how I conceptualize God's invitation to salvation. The question of human freedom and agency comes up often as a justified critique of universalism. Even as I believe we will all come to reconciliation with God in the fullness of time, I do not believe God compels anyone to that state. God is simply always extending the invitation, and eternity is a long time. The door will always be open for us.

What Is the Point?

By far the most frequent question I get online is some version of "If everyone is just going to be saved in the end anyway, what is the point of being a Christian at all?" It comes up so consistently, my friend has been known to jokingly count down days between its occurrence in my comment sections.

I know often the question is coming from a place of genuine confusion, especially given how much we are taught to believe that hell is necessary to Christianity. Nevertheless, it is mind-boggling that so many people do not see the point of embracing a hope in God's reconciling and redeeming love if their faith is not somehow tied to a cosmic "get out of hell free" card. Salvation is not a prize. Salvation is not about getting to sit in a mansion in the sky and playing a harp with a little angel halo. Salvation is about transformation. Salvation is about *living into* the hope that everything that is wrong, broken, and unjust in the world and in ourselves will be made right. If that is our endgame in the scope of human history, why would I not want to be a part of that work of restoration and reconciliation *now*? My faith compels me to put my hope in the teachings of Jesus and to share that hope in the world around me. I do not need the fear of hell to do that.

LOVE

"Simply put, we are not in this alone" (*The Good Place*)

The official NBC *The Good Place* podcast, hosted by actor Marc Evan Jackson, who played the "bad place" demon Shawn, ended every episode with the question "What's good?" It was a pretty open-ended question, eliciting a range of answers from Ted Danson's "the sound of his grandchildren's feet" to more philosophical reflections about the ways that we treat one another. Defining "goodness"—or how we are actually meant to navigate the complexities of life—is a fraught question. *The Good Place* showrunner Michael Schur even expressed his ponderings on the topic in the show's companion book *How to Be Perfect* (I highly recommend the audiobook, which is read by members of the

---

The Good Place, season 2, episode 12, "Somewhere Else," directed by Michael Schur, written by Michael Schur, Kate Gersten, and Cord Jefferson, aired February 1, 2018, on NBC.

show's cast).[1] In the Gospels, Jesus makes it abundantly clear that the one value meant to guide those who would follow him is *love*. Following his Jewish tradition, Jesus identifies the two greatest commandments as the love of God and the love of neighbor: On these two commandments hang all the law and the prophets. On the night before Jesus's arrest and death, Jesus washes his disciples' feet and tells them: "A new command I give you: Love one another. As I have loved you, so you must love one another. By this everyone will know that you are my disciples, if you love one another" (John 13:34–35, NIV). Love may be the foundation of our *goodness*, but—much like goodness itself—love can be a challenging concept to define. In this section, I invite us to wrestle with the concept of love. How do we define the radical nature of love beyond some idea of vague "niceness" or "sentimentality"? How is love connected with our pursuit of justice? What does it mean to live into the reality of love?

The final section explores the dynamics of love specifically in several television comedies. Why, you might ask? At their best, sitcoms present us with a messy ensemble of characters who find their humor not in disparaging one another but in celebrating one another and their relationships. These found families remind us that love, beyond anything else, is a reality that we must live out in connection and communion with others. The moral framework rooted in love can never call us to some sort of individual moral perfection. Personal perfection is as unobtainable as it is undesirable. As Chidi from *The Good Place* reminds us: "Simply put, we are not in this alone."

---

1. Michael Schur, *How to Be Perfect: The Correct Answer to Every Moral Question* (Simon & Schuster, 2022).

"Now we see in a mirror, dimly" (1 Corinthians 13:12): What Is Love?

Defining Love

We often associate the 1 Corinthians 13 passage (love is patient, love is kind, etc.) with its arguable overuse at weddings. The 2005 film *Wedding Crashers* even makes a joke out of how many times the characters hear the passage at the many weddings they illicitly attend. Some readers will also no doubt recognize the framing of "faith, hope, and love" in the passage as inspiration for the order of these reflections. It's worth considering how as a society we have tended to elevate romantic love over other forms of love. Nevertheless, the daily work of love within the covenant of marriage is about much more than romance. The reflection on love in 1 Corinthians, furthermore, is much bigger than marriage. Many of the earliest translations of this passage use the language of charity, not love, which helps us grasp the broader framework of love more clearly. In my own ministry, I find this meditation on love is a much better reflection at funerals, where I often focus on a line at the end of the passage: "For now we see in a mirror, dimly, but then we will see face to face. Now I know only in part; then I will know fully, even as I have been fully known." The manifestations of love that we embody in our relationships are the closest images we have about the nature of God in this mortal life. Yet even our greatest striving to achieve the fullness of that love is but a reflection of the fullness of love that exists in the being of God.

Love Is Simple

Anyone familiar with *The Great British Bake Off* knows the first episode of every season will be cake week. The contestants start with cake and then move to biscuits and eventually more challenging techniques. Bread, pastry, and patisserie weeks are often the most fraught. Whenever I watch *Bake Off*, I end up thinking about Episcopal priest Robert Farrar Capon's *The Supper of the Lamb: A Culinary Reflection*, a brilliant and often funny take on faith and food. When it comes to baking, Fr. Capon talks about the difference between things that are simple and things that are complex. Cake is complex. Pastry is simple. The complexity of cake is ironically what makes it easy to produce. Pretty much anyone can make a cake if you follow even the most basic instructions. Pastry, on the other hand, may be simple, but it requires technique to perfect. You must ensure all your ingredients, and anything that touches them, are ice cold. Work the butter into the flour until you get pea-sized chunks, but be sure not to overwork the dough![1] As much as I love to bake, I still struggle with scones and pie crust. Success in pastry is not about just having the correct instructions but about perfecting skill. This is the reality of love. I sometimes wonder if Jesus looks down on humanity in exasperation and just wants to shout, "I gave you *one job*, how hard

1. Robert Farrar Capon, *The Supper of the Lamb: A Culinary Reflection* (Modern Library, 2002), 155–57.

is that!" Love is simple, and yet we repeatedly mess it up. The work of our lives is the work of learning how to love. Much like learning a skill like pastry, we require teachers and mentors from whom we can learn the craft of loving well. Who in our lives has been that for us? How can we learn from their example? How do we, in turn, model such love for others?

Love Is Strange

Sometimes a TV show comes along, and you are way too aware that you are its target audience. That was my reaction to the 2015 series *Galavant*—a fantasy musical sitcom with music by Disney composing legend Alan Menken. In the first episode, the titular hero Galavant's love Madalena is kidnapped by the wicked King Richard. When Galavant comes to her dashing rescue on her wedding day, it turns out that Madalena has decided that she rather likes life as queen and opts to stay with her kidnapper. As the series unfolds, Galavant ends up on a quest with Isabella, a princess from a neighboring kingdom, ostensibly to prove himself and regain Madalena's love. Along the way, Galavant and Isabella unsurprisingly fall in love, despite their mutual annoyance. They finally confess their feelings in the song "Love Is Strange" with lyrics describing love as rude, annoying, or perhaps even smelly.[2] It is a fairly unsubtle jab at the classic Disney ballads where the leads rhapsodize about the *idea* of love more than the reality of it. Love, frankly, *is* strange in all its forms. Love is not some idealized, abstract concept. Love, romantic or otherwise, does not mean ignoring the annoyances and frustrations of those

---

2. *Galavant*, season 1, episode 6, "Dungeons and Dragon Lady," directed by James Griffiths, written by Kirker Butler, aired January 18, 2015, on ABC, iTunes store.

around us. Instead, love means seeing those around us for who they truly are and having the vulnerability for others to love and accept us. How strange that is!

Love Is Varied 

Young adult fantasy novels can easily fall into the trap of unnecessary love triangles (looking at you Katniss, Gale, and Peeta). Jordan Ifueko's *Raybearer* offers an interesting twist on that trope. *Raybearer* follows Tarisai, who becomes part of the inner council of the crown prince in the Aritsar Empire. The council members are linked to one another through a spiritual "ray" (the prince being the "raybearer").[3] There is so much in this series worth discussing, not least the themes of overthrowing systems of oppression and imagining new ways of structuring society. On a more straightforward character level, though, I appreciate Ifueko's skillful avoidance of the love triangle trap. Tarisai loves crown prince Ekundayo and may expect to be the counselor he chooses to birth his children, but she is romantically drawn to the warrior counselor Sanjeet. Ifueko does not resolve this by having Tarisai pick one of the boys over the other. Instead, Tarisai is allowed to develop her love for both of them in complementary ways: one as her lover, the other as her deepest friend. The fact that Ekundayo eventually acknowledges his asexuality further allows the story to explore the intersections of love among all the members of his council, without them being obscured through a lens of romantic tension. Recognizing that love manifests tangibly in different forms further challenges us to view love as dynamic, not static. Throughout our lives we will embrace different

3. Jordan Ifueko, *Raybearer* (Amulet Books, 2020).

forms of love: in families, friendship, and romance. No one form of love can ever be exhaustive. Love adapts with our different relationships, and one form of love is not a threat to another.

Love Is Punk Rock 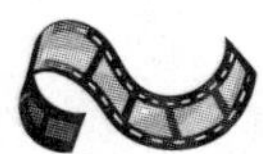

James Gunn deserves many accolades from the geek community, not least because he is responsible for cunningly disguising a *Farscape* reboot as part of the MCU (thank you *Guardians of the Galaxy*). Fandom in general, though, has to thank Mr. Gunn for bringing us a glimmer of hope in human kindness and decency in his 2025 *Superman*. Rejecting other cinematic depictions of Superman over the past decade that portray the Man of Steel as a dispassionate, godlike figure, Gunn, along with actor David Corenswet, offer a vision of Superman as a *man*, one often struggling with what it means to do the right thing. The emotional heart of Gunn's film is the relationship between Lois Lane and Clark Kent/Superman. In a rare move for a superhero film, we get a twelve-minute scene in which Lois and Clark argue over the ethical implications of Superman's actions. When they try to work through their feelings in a later scene, Lois articulates how different they are, identifying herself as a "punk rock" kid who questions everything. She tells Superman: "You think everything and everyone is beautiful," to which he replies, "Maybe that's the real punk rock." The 2025 *Superman* makes it clear in no uncertain terms that Superman's strength is not in his physical body, but in the depth of his radical love for all life (even squirrels). Love is a choice that we make in the face of a world that all too often looks at earnestness and kindness as cringeworthy at best and weak at worst. Heroism is an ongoing process extending kindness and compassion as best we can.

As Superman declares to Lex Luthor: "I wake up every morning and despite not knowing what to do, I put one foot in front of the other and I try to make the best choices I can. I screw up all the time, but that is being human, and that's my greatest strength."[4] I choose to believe that is, indeed, the real punk rock.

Love Is Persevering 

We cannot talk about love without talking about loss. A surprisingly poignant reflection on grief and loss appears in the 2021 Disney+ series *WandaVision*. The series follows Marvel character Scarlet Witch/Wanda Maximoff in the aftermath of losing her lover, the android Vision. Wanda retreats from her grief by creating an alternate reality in the town of Westview, Connecticut. In this reality, Wanda and Vision live out a domestic fantasy progressing through different decades of American family sitcoms. Wanda, who grew up in the fictional Sokovia watching American media, is essentially hiding from her grief in the lie of the American dream. That lie is itself the "big bad" of the series, trapping Wanda and all of Westview in a fictional world where neither pain nor healing can be possible. The ultimate hero is not Wanda but the lesser-known Marvel character Monica Rambeau. Monica struggles with her own grief over the loss of her mother, and her empathy makes her determined to find Wanda. Monica eventually takes it upon herself to enter this curated reality in an attempt to save Wanda, and by extension all of Westview. Rambeau does not save the day with her superpowers but

---

4. *Superman*, directed by James Gunn (2025; Studio Distribution Services, 2025), DVD.

through her capacity to meet Wanda in their shared struggles of grief. Monica's heroism is a profound act of love. In the series finale, the dying Vision comforts Wanda with the beautiful line: "What is grief but love persevering?"[5] Our world pushes us very hard to deny the reality of pain or to "get over" our grief. We honor our love, though, when we allow ourselves to face the inevitability of loss. More importantly, love calls us to have the strength to meet others in their pain, even if it is uncomfortable. Love perseveres.

Love Is Not Afraid

King Herod from the Epiphany story is arguably one of the most tragic characters in the Bible. He is the puppet king of the Jewish people under the oppression of the Roman Empire with very little power or authority. Enter the mysterious "wise men" coming into Jerusalem with the word of some child who will be the new king. While these wise men saw the star in the heavens and were moved with awe to find its meaning, Herod can respond only with the fear of the threat to the meager power he holds. In response, Herod enacts a horrific act of violence, according to Matthew's Gospel, murdering all the boy children in Jerusalem under the age of two. Herod's actions reveal the destructive nature of fear. There are many times in the scriptural texts we are told to *fear not*: the appearances of the angels to Mary and Joseph, the heavenly hosts appearing to the shepherds, etc. The message of God's love is antithetical to fear, in the words of 1 John 4:18: "There is no fear in love, but perfect love casts out fear." Love can certainly make us

5. *WandaVision*, season 1, episode 9, "The Series Finale," directed by Matt Shakman, written by Jac Schaeffer, Peter Cameron, and Mackenzie Dohr, aired March 5, 2021, on Disney+.

afraid. A degree of fear is healthy and natural. What this verse is warning about, though, is the fear that consumes us: the fear that makes our hearts so much smaller. Such fear is destructive. On a personal level, how often does fear keep us from admitting we are wrong or allowing us to show vulnerability in our relationships? We see rising nationalist movements and emboldened white supremacy because so many people fear losing privilege in an increasingly diverse world. Institutions, such as the Church, cling to outdated systems because we fear embracing necessary change. This is the fear that cannot coexist with love.

Love Does No Harm 

In my first year of college chaplaincy, I remember sitting in the chapel with a student who was crying tears of joy because for the first time they realized they did not have to choose between loving God and the fact that they were gay. Students have dubbed my office couch the "queer catharsis couch" thanks to the number of students who have sat on it over the years while processing religious trauma connected to gender and sexuality. A common response from more conservative Christians when challenged to apply Jesus's commandment regarding love of our neighbors to our LGBTQIA+ siblings is that the call to love everyone does not mean condoning "sin." It might be surprising to know that I agree with this up to a point. There are plenty of people whose politics, behaviors, and choices I find abhorrent to the teachings of Jesus, and yet I am still called to love them despite not agreeing with them (or even while finding their beliefs to be harmful). Not only is a person's sexual orientation or gender identity not "sinful," however, it is in fact impossible to love queer and transgender people without affirming who they are as people made in the divine image of God. Being LGBTQIA+ is not some abstract philosophical position. It is part of a person's identity. Theological positions that deny that reality do significant harm. With no exaggeration, we must say that this theology kills. That is why it is so hard for us to hold such unaffirming theologies the deeper we enter into relationships with queer and transgender people. We cannot at the same time love someone and deny who God made them to be. At the very least, we cannot hold those two ideas together without hurting people in the process.

Love Pays It Forward

The movie *Pay It Forward* tells the story of Trevor, a young boy who develops a social experiment for a school project: Whenever someone receives an act of kindness, they should pay that kindness *forward* to three other people. Trevor believes his idea could change the world. In the end, though, Trevor himself is killed in a fight with school bullies, making it an unnecessarily saccharine cinematic experience.[6] I love the *idea* of "paying it forward." This is something I talk about a lot in my work as a college chaplain. I hold tremendous gratitude for the teachers, mentors, and generally supportive people who helped me navigate the challenges of school and vocation. I can never actually pay those people back for all they gave me. I can, however, in a spirit of gratitude, pay that love and support forward to the students I have the privilege of journeying with now. I also make this observation to the students themselves who are sometimes hesitant to accept a free coffee or

6. *Pay It Forward*, directed by Mimi Leder (2000; Warner Home Video, 2001), DVD.

lunch. "This is your time. One day you will be in a position to buy a coffee or a meal for someone." The fact is, love is not a closed system. Love is certainly not a series of transactions that could ever balance out in some cosmic equation. Nevertheless, we can live our lives in gratitude for the love we have received. We can also strive to manifest that love in the world around us. Fully living into such love would certainly be transformational.

"Different choices have always been possible" (N. K. Jemisin, *The Stone Sky*): Love and Justice

What Will We Choose?

Every sci-fi fan owes it to themselves to read N. K. Jemisin's Broken Earth trilogy, beginning with *The Fifth Season.* Jemisin sets the series on "the stillness," a far-future earth that experiences seasons of intensive, destructive weather patterns that disrupt communities for generations. At the center of the series is the race of Orogenes, useful in their supernatural ability to calm the earth and delay those destructive seasons, yet they are feared and dehumanized as a result. Jemisin makes the interesting narrative choices to weave in excerpts from the history of "the stillness" with the rest of the text. As becomes clear by the final chapters, the system of oppression that built community life in the "stillness" was a choice. It was not just a choice made thousands of years ago in the founding of their society, but it is a choice upheld by history, by the lorists (those who hold collective stories), and by the communities that preserve their integrity season after season. In the final chapters of the series, the narrator says: "Imprisonment of the Orogenes was never the only option for ensuring the safety of society. . . .

Different choices have always been possible."[1] The United States is a nation built on white supremacy, but we are not cosmically predestined to remain so. Different choices have always been possible and continue to be possible if we have the courage to face the complicity in white supremacy within ourselves and our institutions, including the Church, and commit ourselves to reparation and reconciliation. This is the active work of love through which we confront a world in need of redemption.

Let Us Make No Peace with Oppression 

In January 2025, I had the amazing opportunity to attend a conference on Christian Zionism at the baptism site of Jesus in Jordan. The gathering involved about sixty academics, theologians, and church leaders from seventeen countries. We began our time together walking the site's pilgrimage route, led by prayer and song at each station along the way. It is a credit to the kindness of Rev. Dr. Mitri Raheb that he invited me to lead a meditation. Being overwhelmed in the moment, I could only think to lead the group in the Taizé chant "Ubi Caritas" (where there is charity, God is present) and to offer this prayer from the Episcopal tradition:

> *Almighty God, who created us in your image: Grant us grace fearlessly to contend against evil and to make no peace with oppression; and, that we may reverently use our freedom, help us to employ it in the maintenance of justice in our communities and among the nations, to the glory of your holy Name; through Jesus Christ our Lord.*[2]

---

1. N. K. Jemisin, *The Stone Sky*, The Broken Earth: Book Three (Orbit, 2017), 395.
2. Book of Common Prayer, 260.

These two texts—the prayer and the Taizé chant—speak to one another. God absolutely is known to us in the presence of love. God *is* love. We must also guard against a bland sort of love that seeks to avoid any type of conflict or controversy. Too often, we conflate the call to love our neighbors, especially in our polarized and divided political landscape, with a call for generic niceness or civility. Love demands that we confront the brokenness of our world. Loving our enemies as Christ compels us to do does not require us to minimize the harm they may have caused or the evil they perpetrated. It does require us to persist in that hope of God's redemptive, not punitive, justice. Love means leaning into the discomfort of our own participation in systems of oppression and opening ourselves to new ways of being. Love must never be divided from justice.

Equality Is Unconditional 

The Midnight Bargain by C. L. Polk is a romance fantasy novel set in a Bridgerton-like marriage mart.[3] Magic is thought to be dangerous to unborn children and, as such, women with magical abilities must wear a special collar to limit their power during the child-bearing years of their marriage. Beatrice Clayborn is a very powerful magic user who wants to protect her magic and to hone her craft as a magician. She consequently seeks to avoid the limitations of marriage, despite pressure from her family. As is the way of romance novels, Beatrice ends up falling in love. Her romantic interest is, essentially, a liberal "nice guy" who promises that *of course* he would let her out of her collar most of the time if they were

3. C. L. Polk, *The Midnight Bargain* (Erewhon, 2020).

married. Marriage to him wouldn't be so bad! Beatrice realizes, however, that such dignity given to her conditionally is still not full human dignity. Such permissions can always be taken away. It is worth considering what Polk says in this book about those of us in positions of privilege. We may be one of the "nice ones," but are we willing to let go of our privilege and dismantle systems of oppression? We must recognize that equality is not some status that the privileged grant to marginalized groups out of their benevolence. More significantly, Polk, a black nonbinary author, clearly intends their work as an encouragement for those who experience oppression to claim their self-worth unambiguously. Women living under patriarchy or people of color living under white supremacy need not wait for those holding privileged identities to affirm their worthiness of love. We do not create the conditions for human dignity: for ourselves or for one another. All we can do is live into our calling of universal, radical love.

The Witness of Queer Christians 

One of the privileges of being a college chaplain was having the opportunity to present a student who had graduated from our campus for ordination as a priest in The Episcopal Church. This student came out as nonbinary during their time at Kenyon, and the dinner event before the ordination was a defiantly joyful gathering of young people who all identified somewhere along the LGBTQIA+ spectrum. That dinner showed me what it means to unapologetically claim your identity in a world that seems determined to rob you of joy. Amid the debates about whether LGBTQIA+ Christians can be fully affirmed in the life of the Church, we often miss the crucial fact that queer Christians are already a vital part of the body of Christ. The queer Christians I have been privileged to know and to pastor have been among some of the most powerfully faithful Christians, precisely because their faith compels them to persist in a Church that all too often challenges their relationships and identities. Even in officially affirming churches like my own Episcopal one, there are still spaces where queer Christians are forced to justify their existence. They are expected to graciously participate in debates where the affirmation of their personhood in the Church is treated as a matter of abstract disagreement and where the Church goes out of its way to make sure that those who hold "traditional" views are not made too uncomfortable. Nevertheless, so many queer Christians persist in loving Jesus and loving the core of the gospel. They are willing to put up with the imperfect mess the Church often is for the sake of their faith. Theirs is a powerful witness of faith and love.

Radical Kindness 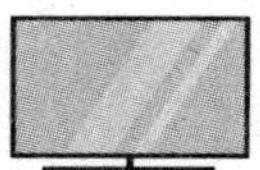

The legendary Fred Rogers made history in 1969 with an episode of *Mister Rogers' Neighborhood* when he invited the recurring character Officer Clemmons to join him in cooling his feet in a wading pool. Mister Rogers's invitation would have been unremarkable, except that Officer Clemmons was black. At the time, swimming pools remained segregated in most of the United States. While it might seem inconsequential fifty years later, we should not lose sight of the radical risk Mister Rogers took in the choice to share a pool with a black man on television. Mister Rogers is often held up as a paragon of kindness and decency. He was himself, after all, a Presbyterian minister who clearly sought to follow Jesus's commandment to love his neighbor. Let us not for a moment think that the love Mister Rogers enacted was bland or weak out of some misplaced idea that practicing radical love meant avoiding controversy or never making people uncomfortable. Acts of radical love are bold. Had social media existed in the 1960s, one can only imagine the number of commentators who would have lined up to offer their hot takes on the scandalous Mister Rogers and his "woke" corruption of children. Years later, in 1993, Mister Rogers and Officer Clemmons met again on set with their wading pool. This time, Mister Rogers knelt and washed Officer Clemmons's feet in a parallel to Jesus's own actions at the last supper. When Clemmons talked about his last appearance on the show, he noted simply the power of the moment: "I am a Black gay man and Fred washed my feet."[4] It can often feel like as individuals we have little power to effect substantive change. In a world where hatred increasingly seems to be the norm, we do well not to underestimate the transformative power of human kindness.

Truth and Reconciliation 

Thanks to over a decade living in Toronto, my children and I both have the honor of being US/Canadian dual citizens. My husband (despite refusing to swear an oath to the queen required for citizenship) has, in response, developed a habit on Canada Day of making my children watch Canadian "Heritage Minutes" on YouTube. These are a series of one-minute documentaries highlighting different aspects of Canadian history. Some of these videos can be ridiculous (we love the real story of how Winnie the Pooh is named after Winnipeg!). They also don't shy away from the more unsavory aspects of Canada's

4. Fred Rogers, quoted in Sara Kettler, "Fred Rogers Took a Stand Against Racial Inequality When He Invited a Black Character to Join Him in a Pool," *Biography*, last updated June 24, 2020, https://www.biography.com/actors/mister-rogers-officer-clemmons-pool.

racist and colonialist history—not least the shame of Canadian residential schools that stole indigenous children from their families for generations. Shortly before I moved back to the United States, the Canadian Truth and Reconciliation Commission completed its report on the Indian Residential Schools. Canada based its process on the work of the apartheid-era Truth and Reconciliation Commission in South Africa, which was largely influenced by Anglican Bishop Desmond Tutu. Much like the United States, Canada has a long way to go to right its national wrongs. However, it cannot hope to do the work of reconciliation without the work of facing the truth of its past. Living into radical love requires radical honesty. That is certainly true in our hope to build genuine beloved communities in our world, but it is also true on the smaller scale of our personal lives. A family cannot make right a history of abuse if the abuser cannot face the harm they have caused. We cannot heal a rift with a friend if we cannot face how we might have hurt them. These are the truths needed for all forms of reconciliation.

Love and Liberation 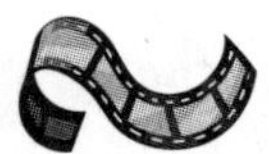

On the surface, the Apple TV series *Severance* seems to be a cautionary tale about corporate culture and alleged work-life balance. Looking deeper, the show asks significant questions about the nature of personhood. Our central character, Mark Scout, has elected to "sever" his personality between his existing "outer" self and his "innie" work self, "Mark S." Due to the severance procedure, Mark S. and his fellow "innies" effectively live imprisoned in the office of Lumon Industries. The story comes to focus on the "innies" pursuit of full personhood. In a dramatic moment, Mark Scout and Mark S. finally confront each other (thanks to clever camerawork and a stellar performance by actor Adam Scott). Mark Scout advocates reintegrating their personalities. Mark S. resists, as the reintegration procedure would leave Mark Scout as the default identity. Mark Scout is a "nice guy." He does not actively want Mark S. to suffer. All the same, Mark Scout ultimately sees Mark S. only as an extension of himself. When Mark S. refuses to go along with Mark Scout's agenda, the latter becomes enraged.[5] There is a warning in these characters: Mark Scout cannot love Mark S. as long as he refuses fully to view Mark S. as a person. Without that love, there can be no liberation for *either* version of Mark. At the heart of our pursuit of justice must be the work of love that is radically committed to affirming the inherent worth of all people. We will always fail in the work of love if we insist on asserting the importance of our own personhood over that of our neighbors. What might we be called to sacrifice to uphold the dignity of all people, particularly the vulnerable and marginalized?

Fie on Fanboys 

One can tell quite a lot about a *Star Wars* fan based on their opinion of Rian Johnson's 2017 *The Last Jedi*.[6] Some of us love that *The Last Jedi* tried to do something new with the *Star Wars* universe. We can destroy the Jedi temple! We can *actually* allow Luke Skywalker to die and pass the proverbial baton to a new generation! After the 2015 reboot *The Force Awakens* raised the question of the mysterious parentage of the new protagonist Rey, *The Last Jedi* made the gamble of suggesting that she was, in fact, related to no one of significance. It was a

5. *Severance*, season 2, episode 10, "Cold Harbor," directed by Ben Stiller, written by Dan Erickson, aired March 21, 2025, on Apple TV+.

6. *Star Wars: The Last Jedi*, directed by Rian Johnson (2017; Lucasfilm, 2019), DVD.

bold choice. Rey did not have to be related to someone powerful or significant to the existing narrative. She could be just as impressive with no name behind her. Sadly, *The Last Jedi* sparked a massive backlash in the *Star Wars* fandom. The 2019 *Rise of Skywalker* reversed many of the story points, including making Rey the granddaughter of Emperor Palpatine. It was clear from the treatment of actors like Daisy Ridley (Rey), John Boyega (Finn), and Kelly Marie Tran (Rose) that much fan backlash was driven by racism and misogyny. Girls are OK in *Star Wars* as long as it is Princess Leia in a bikini and people of color are OK as long as Lando Calrissian stays in his lane. Fanboys throwing tantrums about a more inclusive universe for their space opera is only slightly more absurd than so many white American Christians reacting in defensiveness and anger at the call to build a more inclusive national life in our country. We cannot let the fanboys keep calling the shots in our common life. Shouldn't being fans of fantasy and sci-fi make our imaginations bigger? Pushing the boundaries of inclusion, likewise, allows the boundaries of our faith to expand.

What Is Your Agenda?

A while back, the black author and publishing activist Michael LaBorn shared a question he asks of would-be white allies: Why are you involved in antiracism spaces? Is it because you want to prove, either to yourself or your communities, that you are good people? Or do you engage in the work of dismantling systems of oppression because you truly want a more just world for marginalized people? Do you truly desire the world to change or are you engaged in a project of self-improvement?[7]

---

7. Michael LaBorn, Facebook messenger exchange with author, August 16, 2025. (Original video deleted).

Those questions have stuck with me in the years since our country has faced reckonings of racial justice, attacks on LGBTQIA+ rights, a pandemic that sent economic inequality into overdrive, and the ravages of a genocide in Palestine. Our world is broken. One of the most insidious temptations is always to perform the "right" response to all the injustices we witness. We can be so afraid of having the "wrong" take on a current issue. The arm of internet judgment is swift to those perceived as having transgressed. We also naturally love the dopamine hits that come from likes, shares, and acknowledgments from those who agree with us. The fact remains, however, that if we are engaged in social justice and antiracism work as some kind of self-help project, or out of our own sense of guilt for the privileged identities we may hold, our "allyship" will always be transactional. We will run the risk of drawing back from the work of justice if our contributions are not met with immediate affirmation. Instead, if our commitment to racial justice is born from our genuine commitment to building a better world, we may just find the strength to decenter ourselves and truly commit ourselves to the work of radical love.

"This is the way" (*The Mandalorian*): Living in Love

The Way of Love

My absolute favorite thing on the internet might be a behind-the-scenes picture of Pedro Pascal recording the voice of Mando from *Star Wars: The Mandalorian* while adorably holding a pillow in place of Baby Yoda. *The Mandalorian* is certainly one of the best things to come out of the Star Wars franchise in recent memory, thanks in large part to the relationship developed between the stoic, lone warrior Mando and Grogu/Baby Yoda/"The Child" whom he takes under his wing. Mando's character is committed to the "Way" of the Mandalorian.[1] Among other things, this code of behavior mandates that a Mandalorian never remove their mask. Mando follows this directive, we might say, religiously. In a climactic moment of the series, Grogu is captured. In the process of the rescue operation, Mando is forced into situations where he must face the choice of removing his mask or failing to save Grogu. The choice is agonizing for Mando, but in the moment he realizes that his love for Grogu is a higher calling than his commitment to "The Way." That is an important

---

1. *The Mandalorian*, season 1, episode 1, "Chapter 1: The Mandalorian," directed by Dave Filoni, written by Jon Favreau, aired November 12, 2019, on Disney+.

reminder for all of us. There is no righteousness—no religious perfection—that has significance outside of our love for one another. Love is the higher way.

Dark Isn't Deep

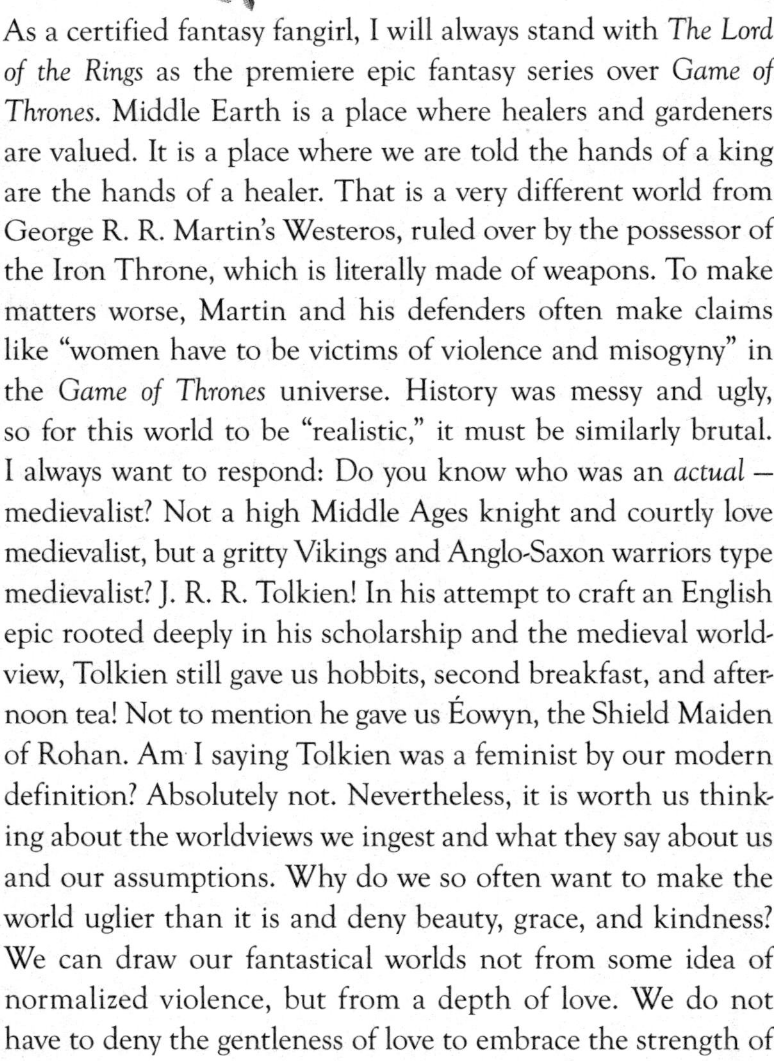

As a certified fantasy fangirl, I will always stand with *The Lord of the Rings* as the premiere epic fantasy series over *Game of Thrones*. Middle Earth is a place where healers and gardeners are valued. It is a place where we are told the hands of a king are the hands of a healer. That is a very different world from George R. R. Martin's Westeros, ruled over by the possessor of the Iron Throne, which is literally made of weapons. To make matters worse, Martin and his defenders often make claims like "women have to be victims of violence and misogyny" in the *Game of Thrones* universe. History was messy and ugly, so for this world to be "realistic," it must be similarly brutal. I always want to respond: Do you know who was an *actual* — medievalist? Not a high Middle Ages knight and courtly love medievalist, but a gritty Vikings and Anglo-Saxon warriors type medievalist? J. R. R. Tolkien! In his attempt to craft an English epic rooted deeply in his scholarship and the medieval worldview, Tolkien still gave us hobbits, second breakfast, and afternoon tea! Not to mention he gave us Éowyn, the Shield Maiden of Rohan. Am I saying Tolkien was a feminist by our modern definition? Absolutely not. Nevertheless, it is worth us thinking about the worldviews we ingest and what they say about us and our assumptions. Why do we so often want to make the world uglier than it is and deny beauty, grace, and kindness? We can draw our fantastical worlds not from some idea of normalized violence, but from a depth of love. We do not have to deny the gentleness of love to embrace the strength of love.

It Feels Like Christmas

The Muppet Christmas Carol is, without doubt, the greatest Christmas movie of all time. What makes the film truly extraordinary is Michael Caine's performance as Ebenezer Scrooge. Caine deserves tremendous praise, first and foremost, for the gravity with which he treats his Muppet costars. On a deeper level, though, Caine brings a vital sadness and loneliness to the character of Scrooge. Through Caine's performance, we see Scrooge as a man who, quite simply, does not know how to love. That lack of love has trapped him in a living hell of his own making. Through the course of his spectral visits, Scrooge learns to see the beauty of love, and he comes to accept that love is something he both wants and is willing to risk. We celebrate Scrooge's redemption not just for the sake of everyone else in his life, such as Tiny Tim, but because we have sympathized with Caine's portrayal of a character that is all too often merely a villain. The film ends with Scrooge sitting down to Christmas dinner with all the other characters we have interacted with through the course of the story, not least the Cratchit family and his nephew Fred. The love Scrooge finds is not an abstract idea, but it is a living reality embodied in the people around him.[2] What does that living reality of love look like as we navigate relationships with our friends and neighbors?

I Am an Islander

The 2017 musical *Come from Away*, written by Canadians Irene Sankoff and David Hein, recounts the true story of the

---

2. *The Muppet Christmas Carol*, directed by Brian Henson (1992; Sony Pictures Home Entertainment, 2012), DVD.

thirty-eight planes carrying seven thousand passengers diverted to the town of Gander, Newfoundland, due to the closure of US airspace following the September 11 terrorist attacks. For five days in the midst of uncertainty, the residents of Gander feed, clothe, and house the so-called "plane people." In one of the most uplifting moments in the show, these plane people decide to blow off steam in a local pub. Through the course of the evening the "come from aways" (visitors to Newfoundland) have the opportunity to participate in a "screech-in" to transform the "come-from-aways" into proper Newfoundlanders. Participants in the ceremony drink a shot of screech (local rum), dress like a Newfoundlander in fishing gear, and kiss a cod.[3] The scene is lively and ridiculous, but as with the rest of the show, it has an underlying poignancy. In a way, the screech-in ceremony feels like a baptism of the "come from aways" into a new life, one defined by radical transformative love. Two characters in the show who are romantic partners are both named Kevin. One Kevin is put off by the absurdity of the ceremony and of Gander itself. He leaves the pub and returns from his whole experience unchanged. The other Kevin finds himself drawn in by the love and hospitality he receives. Not only does he become an honorary Newfoundlander, he returns home as this transformed self. Kevin Tuerff, on whom the fictional counterpart is based, has written and spoken extensively about his experience in Gander and how it changed him. Love is transformation, but we must ask: What are we willing to give up in ourselves to embrace the call of love?

---

3. *Come from Away*, music and lyrics by David Hein and Irene Sankoff, 2017 (Musical Theatre International, 2017).

Our Marks on One Another 

The Invisible Life of Addie LaRue by V. E. Schwab is a haunting novel about a young woman in eighteenth-century France who, while trying to get out of a marriage that she does not want, makes a deal with the devil for freedom and time. As is the devil's way when making deals, he takes Addie quite literally at her word. He curses her to live forever, but never to be remembered by anyone she encounters. Addie goes on to live a cursed, hellish existence: a truly invisible life. She can never form any true relationships and can make no indelible mark on the world. As Addie navigates her life, she discovers creative ways to form connections with the people she encounters.[4] Addie's circumstance serves as a catalyst for a meditation on life and what it means to live in genuine relationships with others. Human relationships are complicated, messy, and also beautiful. What does it mean to be human? Can we isolate our lives from the impact we make on those around us? One might say those impressions we leave on one another are the tangible work of love. Through love, we are, in fact, bound to the people in our lives. The bonds of love are not a prison, but they are indeed the basis for meaning and purpose. Love is simultaneously connection and freedom. Love means embracing life with those around us that will involve sin, pain, and hurt, but also joy and abundance. What are the marks those we love have made on our lives? How do we wish to impact the world that we inhabit?

---

4. V. E. Schwab, *The Invisible Life of Addie LaRue* (Tor, 2020).

Curbing Consumption 

In her young adult Scholomance trilogy, Naomi Novik comes up with one of the most disturbing fantasy monsters: the so-called "maw-mouths."[5] These are horrific beings made up of just insatiable hunger, who consume without any end and cannot be killed. Victims of the maw-mouth do not die but live on as part of the creature's endless appetite. Novik does not just make the maw-mouths creepy for their own sake. The monsters are thematically critical to the series. The books take place in a world where magical youth are particularly susceptible to malevolent forces. Families are desperate for their children to survive to adulthood. Powerful and privileged people, consequently, pool their resources into "conclaves," leaving the vulnerable unprotected. What begins as a natural, understandable drive of parents wanting to protect their children grows into a malicious system in which they are willing to sacrifice others to achieve that security. Those who *have* much continue to take yet more, never able to be full. Novik's books are a very powerful social commentary, particularly for our world right now. We are seduced through media, advertisements, influencers, and so on to always feel as though to be *enough* we must consume more and more. Allowing ourselves to feel *satisfied* goes against so much of our economic and social conditioning. Much like the characters in Novik's books, some of our patterns of consumption emerge from a very natural desire to provide for our families and our children—to ensure their security and happiness. In this way, our love can become twisted and corrupt. We cannot provide

5. Naomi Novik, *A Deadly Education* (Del Rey, 2020).

for ourselves or those we love when we allow our culture of insatiable consumption to destroy the world around us. What might it mean for us to embrace being satisfied and to move from a mindset of scarcity to one of abundance born from love?

No One Is Alone

One of my musical theater hot takes is that *Into the Woods* is actually pretty uplifting. That may seem an odd opinion, but bear with me. The show is a mash-up of classic fairy-tale characters who all go "into the woods" in pursuit of their separate wishes, most notably the Baker and Baker's Wife, who long for a child. The first act ends with their stories tied up in a neat bow: The Baker and his wife have their child. Cinderella and Rapunzel find their respective princes. Jack brings home treasure from the top of the beanstalk. In Act Two: It all goes wrong! Or does it? Clearly, some unfortunate events take place. The wife of the giant killed by Jack comes to seek her revenge on our heroes. Cinderella's prince enjoys a dalliance with the Baker's Wife, who is promptly killed by our giantess. The characters argue with one another about who holds most blame for their current circumstances. In the end, however, rather than continuing their own individualistic agendas, the characters do come together to fight the giant.[6] Act One may wrap up with a superficial "happy ending," but the actions of the characters each seeking only their own desires directly cause the catastrophes that emerge in Act Two. As we see, the

6. *Into the Woods*, music and lyrics by Stephen Sondheim, 1987 (Musical Theatre International, 2009).

wishes the characters so desperately sought did not actually satisfy. This is most delightfully depicted in the princes' song of the respective *agony* of unrequited love that loses its luster once attained. We live in a world that tells us to chase our bliss and pursue our wishes! That is the core of the American dream, after all. How has that worked out for us? How has that worked out for the world? We do well to remember, as Cinderella sings to comfort Jack: We are not alone. We change the world by realizing our wishes can only be truly fulfilled in love and community with one another.

I Hope We Choose Love 

Without a doubt one of the most transformative books I have ever read is *I Hope We Choose Love: A Trans Girl's Notes from the End of the World*, written in 2019 by Kai Cheng Thom. Those of us in progressive communities believe that love and justice are interconnected. Despite that, anyone who has spent any time in social justice spaces knows how harsh and punitive they can be. Perfection can be demanded from would-be allies, allowing little room for growth or repentance. We delight in "calling out" rather than "calling in." I sometimes find progressive spaces troubling when holding the right beliefs or knowing the latest trending terminology is valued above the tangible work of love in community. Kai Cheng Thom's work is powerful because it is an unapologetic call for a world of radical liberation, while also talking straightforwardly about the failed promises in many justice movements. Now, years after she wrote them, her words feel truer than ever: "We must encourage love—love that is radical, love that digs deep. . . . We live in poison. The Planet is dying. We can choose to consume one another, or we can choose love. Even in the midst of despair, there is always a choice. I hope we choose love."[7] I wonder how it might transform our lives and relationships if we truly understood the work of love as something that we must actively *choose*. The ongoing work of love is also not just a choice we make once, but a reality we are called to choose every day.

The Literal Heart of Jesus

Fun fact: My church is home to the literal heart of Jesus.

OK. Not *literally*. John Green did, however, base the layout of the cruciform church in his 2012 novel *The Fault in Our Stars* on Kenyon College's Church of the Holy Spirit, including the room directly under the altar. In Green's novel, this room hosts the teenage cancer support group and, given its location, becomes known as "the literal heart of Jesus."[8] It has not been uncommon for prospective students or other campus visitors to come by the church office asking where they can find "the literal heart of Jesus" and it always sparks a fun conversation about John Green's connection to Kenyon and our parish in particular. While the "Literal Heart of Jesus" idea is played off in the novel as a silly quirk of an overly earnest cancer support group facilitator, I like to think there is power in the idea of our church holding the heart of Jesus between us. A more substantive physical feature of the church is the "collegiate" style arrangement of the pews. Rather than being organized in front-to-back rows all facing the altar, the

7. Kai Cheng Thom, *I Hope We Choose Love: A Trans Girl's Notes from the End of the World* (Arsenal Pulp Press, 2019), 91.

8. John Green, *The Fault in Our Stars* (Penguin Random House, 2012), 17.

arrangement of the pews forces members of the congregation to look at one another. As I write this, I can hear a liturgical traditionalist declaring that the purpose of worship is orientation to God, not to other people. A big part of me gets that. At the same time, I remember that we cannot love God if we do not allow ourselves to love those around us. All our meditations on love come down to this truth: Love does not exist in the abstract. The single greatest witness to God's presence in the world is the people who bear God's divine image. In loving one another, we invite the literal heart of Jesus to be present among us. This, quite simply, is the heart of Jesus we are called to share in the world.

"We talk it through as a crew!" (*Our Flag Means Death*): Love in Laughter

Sitcom Sanctification

There's been a recent noticeable trend in sitcoms to find laughter in human goodness: shows like *The Good Place*, *Schitt's Creek*, and *Ted Lasso*. By virtue of the genre, sitcoms are always going to explore the foibles of a mixed group of individuals. Done well, these shows invite us to see the goodness born out even in the complexities of human relationships. More significantly, these feel-good sitcoms break down the idea that this goodness is anything that could ever be, or should ever be, achieved individualistically. All of these shows present beautiful stories of healing and redemption that are achieved through relationship, community, and communion. When we think about holiness or some idea of sanctification, especially as we reflect on people lifted up by the Church as examples of sainthood, the last thing we should be thinking about is a bunch of morally perfect people. There is a reason, after all, that the Church confesses faith in a "communion of saints." Sainthood is about

---

Our Flag Means Death, season 1, episode 9, "Act of Grace," directed by Bertie Ellwood and Amber Templemore, written by David Jenkins, Yvonne Zima, and Eliza Jiménez Cossio, aired March 24, 2022, on HBO Max.

a communal reality that we are called into, first by opening ourselves up to the transformative love of God, and then by bearing witness to that love in our relationships with one another. Holiness is a reality we can only embrace in communion with God and one another. Maybe sitcoms also demonstrate for us that the holiness of community need not be an overly serious business. Love can be ridiculous. In the words of *Schitt's Creek*'s Moira Rose: "Let us celebrate that."[1]

Evangelism and Gay Pirates

Starring New Zealand comedic icons Rhys Darby and Taika Waititi, *Our Flag Means Death* centers on the real-life "Gentleman Pirate" Stede Bonnet and his (historical) relationship with the fearsome "Blackbeard," Edward Teach. Along the way Ed and Stede find not only love but healing of their insecurities. A kind of evangelism is at work in how the characters in Ed and Stede's crew inspire one another to become better people. There is no better example of such transformation than the character of Izzy Hands, who begins the story as Blackbeard's first mate. Progressive Christians can understandably find the idea of evangelizing quite off-putting. What if we put evangelism in the framework of the redemption of Izzy Hands in the second season of *Our Flag Means Death* and the beauty of found family? Spoilers ahoy! Izzy was not pleasant in season one, actively working to sabotage Ed and Stede's relationship. He encouraged the crueler parts of Ed's "Blackbeard" persona to serve his own interests. We see Izzy dramatically change in season two, however, largely through

1. *Schitt's Creek*, season 4, episode 7, "The Barbecue," directed by Sturla Gunnarsson, written by David West Read, aired March 6, 2018, on CBC Television.

the efforts of the crew. No one gives Izzy an ultimatum: "You better apologize and fix yourself if you want to be accepted as part of our crew." They *loved* him instead. When Izzy loses his leg, the crew uses the masthead of the ship to make him a proper pirate peg leg.[2] Being embraced into that reality allowed for Izzy to change and repent. The call for those of us who seek to follow Jesus and the call to be "fishers of people" is not about proselytizing or getting people to accept a particular belief system. It is about asking *us* if we believe the good news about the God who desires reconciliation and the redemption of the world. The more we live into that reality of love, the more we would want to share it with others.

Be Curious, Not Judgmental 

Ted Lasso begins with the, frankly ridiculous, premise of an American college football coach moving to England to manage a premiere league soccer team. From that unlikely point, the show goes on to explore the extraordinary power of kindness and basic decency. One of the most satisfying scenes in the first season happens when the loveable Ted reveals his hidden skill at darts. Ted has been taunted by the villainous Rupert, former owner of Ted's team, the Richmond Greyhounds, and played to smarmy perfection by Anthony Steward Head. In a moment of triumph, Ted tells the story of being taught to play darts as a child by his father, besting the villainous Rupert to the cheers of the gathered crowd. With his winning shot, Ted shares the Walt Whitman quotation "Be curious, not

---

2. *Our Flag Means Death*, season 2, episode 4, "Fun and Games," directed by Andrew DeYoung, written by David Jenkins, Eliza Jiménez Cossio, and John Mahone, aired October 12, 2023, on HBO Max.

judgmental,"[3] a not-so-subtle dig at Rupert's arrogance in assuming the American Ted's lack of skills at the popular British pub game. This saying becomes something of a thesis statement for the series. What does it mean to approach one another with curiosity rather than judgment? Ted himself, with all his hidden depths, obviously illustrates this. We might also look at the anger-driven, profanity-spewing Roy Kent, whose capacity for leadership lies beneath the surface. Or even the seemingly mild-mannered Nathan, who has deep resentments born from childhood pain. There is so much harm being done today by those whose first impulse is judgment, not curiosity about the world and the people around us. None of us are who we seem on the surface, in both good and bad ways. How might our lives and our world be different if we truly leaned into curiosity born out of love?

Our Saving Grace 

In the opening episode of *Schitt's Creek*, we meet the wealthy Rose family having their possessions seized by the government. The one asset remaining to them being the town of Schitt's Creek, purchased by the family patriarch as a gag gift for his son David. As they prepare to uproot their privileged life of luxury to move into the titular town, the government agent says in passing, "This town may just be your saving grace."[4] How true that statement becomes over the course of the series! *Schitt's Creek* can be seen as a show about the theological concept of

3. *Ted Lasso*, season 1, episode 8, "The Diamond Dogs," directed by Declan Lowney, written by Leann Bowen, Brett Goldstein, and Phoebe Walsh, aired September 18, 2020, on Apple TV+.

4. *Schitt's Creek*, season 1, episode 1, "Our Cup Runneth Over," directed by Jerry Ciccoritti, written by Dan Levy, aired January 13, 2015, on CBC Broadcasting.

prevenient grace, the idea that God's grace goes before us and enables our reconciliation to God and neighbor. At first glance, the members of the Rose family are all pretty insufferable. Moira is selfish and egotistical. Johnny is impatient and self-important. David is aloof and image-obsessed. Alexis is a shallow socialite. The joy of *Schitt's Creek* is watching the Rose family receive love from the admittedly also messy and imperfect members of their new community, despite being absolutely unworthy of it. As a result of such grace, they grow into, perhaps not fundamentally transformed, but *better* versions of themselves. This is most evident in the character of David, in both his friendship with hotel clerk Stevie and romance with business partner-turned-husband Patrick. David hides deep woundedness under a seemingly selfish, shallow exterior. He longs to be loved but fears the risk of vulnerability. Allowing himself to be loved in all of his flaws and idiosyncrasies allows him to become capable of kindness and even occasional selflessness. His story is a beautiful distillation of the truth that receiving love makes us capable of giving love.

Abbott Apocalypse

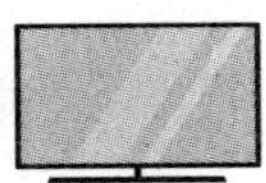

What do the Apocalypse and *Abbott Elementary* have in common? It can be easy to feel that we are living in apocalyptic times, in the truest sense of the term *apocalypse*, which means "unveiling." Wars, pandemics, and overwhelming election cycles continue to reveal how much of our world is broken. It's valid to be frustrated with incremental progress and what feels like half measures by pragmatists. But for all that it is essentially a workplace sitcom about an under-resourced Philadelphia public school, *Abbott Elementary* manages to offer some pointed commentary on urgency and persistence when it comes to addressing systemic challenges. On one end of the spectrum, we have the idealistic Janine, a young teacher who directs boundless energy confronting head-on every problem of injustice or inequality she encounters. We also see the disillusionment that results when that change does not happen as she earnestly hopes. The show contrasts Janine with seasoned veteran teachers Barbara and Melissa, doing faithful work year after year for their students in less-than-ideal circumstances.[5] Janine, Barbara, and Melissa all love their students equally. Perhaps we need both forms of love. As we confront the brokenness of the world that is being unveiled, let us embrace the passion of youthful optimism and the steady, persevering love born of experience.

Eternal Salvation and Chocolate Biscuits 

Starring comedian Dawn French, *The Vicar of Dibley* started in 1994, shortly after the ordination of women in the Church of England. It follows the antics of Geraldine Granger, titular vicar of the country village of Dibley and the eccentric cast of characters that makes up her parish. One of my favorite exchanges in the series happens as Geraldine asks the down-to-earth farmer Owen to help her take her groceries out of her car:

> *"What's in it for me?"*
> *"Eternal salvation?"*
> *"Anything more, you know, unnebulous?"*
> *"A chocolate hobnob?"*[6]

---

5. *Abbott Elementary*, created by Quinta Brunson, aired in 2021, on ABC.

6. *The Vicar of Dibley*, season 2, episode 1, "Engagement," directed by Dewi Humphreys, written by Richard Curtis and Paul Mayhew-Archer, aired December 26, 1997, on BBC One (BBC, 2020), DVD.

With this promise assured, Owen happily helps the vicar with her groceries. It is a ridiculous moment, but I find it so pastorally relatable. The fact is, we human beings are tangible, messy creatures who live in a tangible, messy world. I certainly believe in the promises of eternal salvation and the hope for the restoration of the world. I also think we can be honest about the fact that orienting ourselves toward eternal rewards can be less motivating than what we experience in this life. Small, tangible, meaningful acts of love toward one another have the power to be transformative. It is from these meaningful moments that we allow God to work through us to bring about reconciliation in our world and in our communities. We all need the gift of a chocolate biscuit now and then, and that's OK.

Bye-Bye Li'l Moxie 

Given my current status as a chaplain and parish priest in a small rural village where my husband is also the mayor, I sometimes feel like I live in the perfect crossover of *The Vicar of Dibley* and *Parks and Recreation*. That really hit home in the summer of 2022 when our community mourned the loss of our unofficial mascot Moxie the cat, who was known to ride on student backpacks and occasionally wander into the chapel in the middle of services. Moxie's role on our campus was even celebrated in an issue of *The Atlantic*. If you know anything about *Parks and Recreation*, Moxie was our version of Li'l Sebastian, the tiny horse whose beloved icon status brought together the idiosyncratic residents of Pawnee, Indiana. We may not have had Andy Dwyer to sing "5,000 Candles in the Wind" as he did for the passing of Li'l Sebastian, but there was a funeral for Moxie attended by people from throughout the campus and village to pay their respects to our feline friend.[7] For all its comedic exaggerations, *Parks and Recreation* does accurately reflect that lived relationships in community rely on silly but meaningful things that we hold in common. We live in a world where we are increasingly pushed toward isolation, where we are not encouraged to get to know our neighbors and communities. In this moment, markers of community like Moxie the Cat or the fictional Li'l Sebastian can be transformative for us. We can only love our neighbors if we actually know and build a sense of community with one another.

The Hardest Person to Love  

While more of a musical comedy than a situational comedy, the tragically underappreciated series *Crazy Ex-Girlfriend* is worthy of a shout-out. Rachel Bloom stars as Rebecca Bunch, a New York lawyer struggling with multiple mental health issues, who uproots her life to follow her teenage ex-boyfriend to West Covina, California. As a former "theater kid," Rebecca sees her life as a musical. This leads to some truly great television as she uses different genres and styles of music to reflect on aspects of the human experience ranging from the ridiculous to the profound. One song that to this day hits a little close to home is "a song of self-indulgent self-loathing" called "You Stupid B*tch."[8] The title pretty much says it all, as Rebecca croons a lounge number listing everything she hates

---

7. *Parks and Recreation*, season 3, episode 16, "Li'l Sebastian," directed by Dean Holland, written by Dan Goor, Katie Dippold, and Harris Wittels, aired May 19, 2011, on NBC.

8. *Crazy Ex-Girlfriend*, season 1, episode 11, "That Text Was Not Meant for Josh!," directed by Daisy von Scherler Mayer, written by Elisabeth Kiernan Averick, Rene Gube, and Sono Patel, aired February 8, 2016, on the CW.

about herself. The song is so relatable because, quite honestly, sometimes the hardest person for us to love is ourselves. Loving ourselves might seem less important than loving others, but as Rebecca's journey in *Crazy Ex-Girlfriend* goes on to show, when we are rooted in self-loathing we do not actually have the capacity to live in loving relationships with others. Most importantly, if we cannot bring ourselves to believe we are worthy of unconditional love, how can we truly believe so of others?

"The Reason Is Friends"[9] 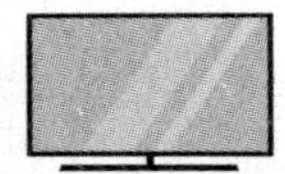

As is no doubt clear by this point, if there is one piece of media that best captures my theology and view of how we are called to live in the world, *The Good Place* would be it! Fair warning: If you have not watched the show's first season, please go do so now before we continue. You've seen it? Great! Let's move on. Suffice it to say the show creator, Michael Schur, established a universe where an elaborate ethical point system determined whether people ended up in the "Good Place" or the "Bad Place" after death. Through its central cast of characters, led by Kristen Bell's Arizona dirtbag Eleanor Shellstrop, the show invites the audience to explore how we understand the concept of goodness. Doug Forcett, the Alberta stoner, had a vision in which he fully articulated 92 percent of the moral truth in the universe, making him the person in human history who most understood the afterlife. When we finally meet him in the later seasons of the show, however, he is a neurotic mess. Doug lives his life in an obsessive attempt to maximize his ethical

---

9. *The Good Place*, season 2, episode 6, "Janet and Michael," directed by Dean Holland, written by Kate Gersten, Cord Jefferson, and Andrew Law, aired October 26, 2017, on NBC.

point total. Not only does this make him miserable, we learn that even Doug's meticulous efforts have not qualified him for the good place.[10]

We can make similar observations about Chidi, the moral philosophy professor in the main cast who manages to alienate everyone in his life through his anxiety around making the best ethical choices. Moral perfection according to some elaborate scoring metric is something none of us can achieve on our own. As both Chidi and Doug Forcett show, moreover, even if such individualistic perfection were possible, it is not a particularly desirable end goal. The quest for moral perfection leads us to be obsessively focused inward. Rather, throughout the series, the characters achieve goodness the more they lean into their relationships and learn from one another. "Goodness" can only be achieved through the reality of love nurtured in communion and community with those around us. While the philosopher Jean-Paul Sartre coined the phrase "Hell is other people," *The Good Place* makes the opposite claim: *Heaven* is other people. Perhaps Ted Danson's character, Michael, summed it up best when he declared the reasons driving his behavior: "The reason is friends." What better reason can guide us as we navigate the complexities of our lives and bear witness to God's divine love in our messy, broken, but also wonderful world?

---

10. *The Good Place*, season 3, episode 8, "Don't Let the Good Life Pass You By," directed by Dean Holland, written by Andrew Law, Cord Jefferson, and Daniel Schofield, aired November 15, 2018, on NBC; *The Good Place*, season 3, episode 9, "Janet(s)," directed by Morgan Sackett, written by Josh Siegal, Dylan Morgan, and Cord Jefferson, originally aired December 6, 2018, on NBC, iTunes store.

IN CONCLUSION

In true nerd fashion, allow me to end with a reflection on J. R. R. Tolkien's concept of the *eucatastrophe*, or:

> *The consolation of fairy-stories, the joy of the happy ending: or more correctly of the good catastrophe, the sudden joyous turn. . . . It does not deny the existence of dyscatastrophe, of sorrow and failure: the possibility of these is necessary to the joy of deliverance; it denies (in the face of much evidence, if you will) universal final defeat and in so far is evangelium, giving a fleeting glimpse of Joy, Joy beyond the walls of the world, poignant as grief.*[1]

The eucatastrophe takes many forms—shout-out to Jodi McAlister's rom-com *An Academic Affair*, where one of the main characters makes her scholarly work applying Tolkien's euchatastrophe to literature from romance novels to *Anne of Green Gables*![2] For Tolkien, though, the greatest eucatastrophe is the Christian story of Christ's birth and resurrection, which Tolkien describes as "a fairy-story, or a story of a larger kind which embraces all the essence of fairy stories."[3]

---

1. J. R. R. Tolkien, "On Fairy-stories," in *The Monsters and the Critics and Other Essays*, ed. Christopher Tolkien (Harper Collins, 1997), 153.
2. Jodi McAlister, *An Academic Affair* (Atria, 2025).
3. Tolkien, "On Fairy-stories," 155.

I have long taken great comfort from Tolkien's description of joy. The eucatastrophe is a good catastrophe, but it is still catastrophic. We aren't called into a naive joy that denies the sorrow and confusion and hurt that we so often carry with us. The Christian faith does not just proclaim a God who triumphed over death and came out the other side in glory in some distant regal majesty. What we celebrate at Easter is the promise of a God who triumphed over the power of sin and death, who also came out the other side bearing the scars of his own crucifixion (John 20:20). Our faith teaches that our resurrected God encounters us in our brokenness and vulnerability. I love that in the Easter Gospels, we see the resurrected Christ appearing not to people who already believe he rose from the dead. Jesus appears to the scared, the confused, the doubting. I like to think not having our act together is a feature, not a bug, in the journey of faith.

It's worth remembering that the Christian story did not end with the eucatastrophe of the resurrection. If I could encourage you to take one thing from the eclectic mix of reflections included in this book, it is to pay attention to the little eucatastrophes through which glimpses of God break into the messiness of our lives. There are no rules for when or how God might show up. Experiencing and sharing in the love of God definitely does not mean we have all the answers! When our world feels heavy and far from our hope of justice and liberation for all people, we remember that our stories are still being written. And just maybe, each of us has a part to play in the eucatastrophe for which we are eagerly waiting.

ACKNOWLEDGMENTS

Writing is at once a very solitary endeavor and also the product of so many influences. I am profoundly grateful to my editors Katherine Lim and Fiona Hallowell, who were committed to successfully adapting my online "60 Second Sermons" to book form. Katherine was a phenomenal colleague, always ready to offer encouragement and feedback (not to mention more reading suggestions in our Google Docs comments).

The Nerdy Priest would not exist if my beloved student Ceci Rodriquez had not stolen my phone to make my TikTok account and film my first-ever video while we cooked Shrove Tuesday pancakes in February 2020. The TikTok community (especially our #ProgressiveClergy squad) truly changed my life. I owe the platform I have to the many people who liked and shared my content, and to those who asked challenging questions that forced me to sharpen or change my theological convictions. I must especially acknowledge my friends Mary Bohall and Matthew Benfield, who have become trusted confidants and sounding boards as I developed this project.

I am privileged to be part of the wonderful community in Gambier, Ohio, and at Kenyon College. The congregation of Harcourt Parish deserves tremendous credit for putting up with my nerdy sermon illustrations for a full decade and for supporting my online ministry. As a priest I could not ask for a more supportive church to serve. Thank you to the several friends and colleagues who offered me advice or feedback at various stages of the project: Clint Bailey, Bridget Coffey, Elizabeth Dark, Leah Romanelli DeJesus, Bob Milnikel, Jamie Lyn Smith, Anna Woofenden, and Natalie Wright. Thank you as well to my students Oliver Kreeger, Zan Lapp, and Elizabeth Redmond for invaluable editorial assistance and feedback. Everyone should have a great local bookstore, and I have to give a shout-out to Paragraphs in Mount Vernon, Ohio, for my steady supply of material for TikTok content and sermon illustrations.

Throughout the book I reference a number of friends, colleagues, and mentors who shaped my faith over the years. There are too many to list again here, but my gratitude is no less sincere. A reference in these acknowledgments seems hardly sufficient thanks to my husband, Leeman, for his support of this project, from taking on the lion's share of parenting responsibilities to proofreading and commenting on multiple drafts. You're simply the best.